FAITH AND
REVELATION

By the Same Author

Scripture for Meditation:

THE INFANCY NARRATIVES
PHILIPPIANS
OUR DIVINE MASTER
COLOSSIANS
CHRISTIAN DEUTERONOMY

Householder Commentaries:

GALATIANS

Scripture for Meditation: 6

FAITH AND REVELATION

by John Bligh

ALBA · HOUSE   NEW · YORK

SOCIETY OF ST. PAUL, 2187 VICTORY BLVD., STATEN ISLAND, NEW YORK 10314

Bligh, John.
  Faith and revelation.
  (Scripture for meditation ; 6)
  1. Faith—Meditations. 2. Revelation—Meditations.
I. Title. II. Series.
BV4637.B54   1975   234'.2   74-31319
ISBN 0-8189-0311-2

1975 EDITION

SCRIPTURE FOR MEDITATION: Volume 6
Faith and Revelation

Originally published by St. Paul Publications, Slough, England.

Nihil Obstat: Gerard E. Roberts, Censor.
Imprimatur: +Charles Grant, Bishop of Northampton,
24 April 1972.

© Copyright 1972 St. Paul Publications.

Printed in the United States of America by the Fathers
and Brothers of the Society of St. Paul at Alba House,
2187 Victory Blvd., Staten Island, New York 10314,
as part of their communications apostolate.

Current Printing: (last digit)
9 8 7 6 5 4 3 2 1

CONTENTS

Foreword	7
Faith in God	9
Faith in Christ	12
Why Believe in Christ?	16
Faith in God and Faith in Christ	19
Faith as a Gift	22
Revelation as Liberation	25
Revelation as Salvation	28
Faith in Moses and Faith in Christ	32
God is revealed as God of Peace	35
The Sages of Revelation	38
Moments of Revelation	42
Revealed Truths Natural and Supernatural	45
Faith drives out Fear	48
The Certainty of Faith	51
A Covenant stronger than Death	54
Faith and Honour	57
The Disciple and His Master	60
The Obscurity of Faith	63
A Hidden Epiphany	67
Difficulties and Doubts	70
Understanding too is a Gift	74
Faith is a Victory	78
Self-Deflating Wisdom	81
Revelation of Justice and Sinfulness	85
Faith and Morality	88
Faith Working through Charity	91
A Kingdom of Priests	94
Faith in the Priesthood	97
Faith in the Church	100
Believing and Seeing	103
The Gift of Authority	106
Faith in God's Promises	110
Faith and Vision	113
Bible passages used	117

Acknowledgement

The Bible text in this publication is from the Revised Standard Version Bible, Catholic Edition, copyrighted © 1965 and 1966 by the Division of Christian Education of the National Council of the Churches of Christ in the U.S.A., and used by permission.

Foreword

This sixth book of *Scripture for Meditation* contains a series of reflections on various aspects of faith and revelation. What is meant by 'faith' and by 'revelation' cannot well be summed up in theological definitions. When we have said that faith is a supernatural gift of God by which we believe without doubting whatever God has revealed, and that revelation is the communication of truth from God to man, we have hardly begun to explore these concepts. They receive clearer definition by being related to a network of cognate concepts, such as knowledge, certainty, obscurity, fear, strength, liberation, honour, disappointment, morality, mediation, interdependence, understanding, vision and so on. Some of these relationships are mapped out in the following pages, for the benefit of anyone who cares to read them.

John Bligh

1

FAITH IN GOD

God creates man

God said, "Let the earth bring forth living creatures according to their kinds: cattle and creeping things and beasts of the earth according to their kinds." And it was so. And God made the beasts of the earth according to their kinds and the cattle according to their kinds, and everything that creeps upon the ground according to its kind. And God saw that it was good.

Then God said, "Let us make man in our image, after our likeness; and let them have dominion over the fish of the sea, and over the birds of the air, and over the cattle, and over all the earth, and over every creeping thing that creeps upon the earth." So God created man in his own image, in the image of God he created him; male and female he created them. And God blessed them, and God said to them, "Be fruitful and multiply, and fill the earth and subdue it; and have dominion over the fish of the sea and over the birds of the air and over every living thing that moves upon the earth."

The Lord God took the man and put him in the garden of Eden to till it and keep it. And the Lord God commanded the man saying, "You may freely eat of every tree of the garden; but of the tree of the knowledge of good and evil you shall not eat, for in the day that you eat of it you shall die." *(Gen 1:24-28;2:15-17)*

God cares for man

"Look at the birds of the air; they neither sow nor reap nor gather into barns, and yet your heavenly Father feeds them. Are you not of more value than they? And which of you by being anxious can add one cubit to his span of life? And why are you anxious about clothing? Consider the lilies of the field, how they grow; they neither toil nor spin; yet I tell you, even Solomon in all his glory was not arrayed like one of these. But if God so clothes the grass of the field, which today is alive and tomorrow is thrown into the oven, will he not much more clothe you, O men of little faith?"

(Mt 6:26-30)

Reflection

In this passage from the Sermon on the Mount, Christ our Lord is urging his disciples to have faith in God. He is also showing us what it means to have faith in God. He does not teach them how to reason their way to belief in a necessary, eternal being. He does not argue, as a philosopher might, that the world is full of fleeting, transient beings that come into existence and pass away; but none of these can explain its own existence; therefore above and beyond the stream of fleeting things there must be a necessary and eternal being from whom all other beings have their origin. This argument is of value to philosophers and intellectuals—Tolstoy was convinced by it; but most people find more help in our Lord's words about the birds and the flowers—if we open our eyes, we can see in them a reflection of God's love and concern. Our own being is much more wonderful—our body, and still more our mind, with its fantastic power of discovery and organization. Cannot we, then, see in our own persons, in our 'gifts' and 'talents', the evidence of God's love?

To believe in God is to believe in a Creator who is good, who loves even the least of his creatures with an

unpossessive, contemplative love. He sees that they are good or can become good, and loves them and cares for them. This is one of the lessons of the reading from Genesis: that God is the creator of all that is good in us, and loves us as his creatures. To 'believe in God', for a Jew, a Christian or a Muslim, is to believe in a God of a certain kind: one who created the world and guides our lives in justice and love—a God to whom we can entrust ourselves, upon whose Fatherly providence we can rely.

There is a helpful passage in the Book of Job, where Job's wife tempts him to abandon his faith in God. She does not say to him: 'Can't you conclude from all these sufferings that God does not exist?' She tempts him to abandon his faith in God—not to doubt God's existence, but to doubt his love. (In the same way, Satan tempted Eve in paradise to suspect God of jealousy and deception.) Job's wife says: 'Curse God and die!' meaning: 'Provoke him, and he will finish you off.' Job shows the greatness of his faith by refusing to doubt God's goodness, even though he cannot understand: 'The Lord has given, the Lord has taken away: blessed be the name of the Lord!' That is the true act of religious faith—humbly to believe in the goodness of God, even in spite of appearances to the contrary—to abandon one's life into God's hands, saying: 'Take, O Lord, and receive my memory, understanding and will; take them, and guide them by your grace.'

Prayer

Heavenly Father, Creator of the universe, who dost rule our lives in justice and love, we give thanks for your loving providence and protection, and we ask for the Spirit of your Son, so that we may live in perfect obedience to your will. Through the same Jesus Christ your Son our Lord, who lives and reigns with you in the unity of the Holy Spirit, God, for ever and ever.

2

FAITH IN CHRIST

Our Future Judge

Paul, standing in the middle of the Areopagus, said: "Men of Athens, I perceive that in every way you are very religious. For as I passed along, and observed the objects of your worship, I found also an altar with this inscription, 'To an unknown god.' What therefore you worship as unknown, this I proclaim to you. The God who made the world and everything in it, being Lord of heaven and earth, does not live in shrines made by man, nor is he served by human hands, as though he needed anything, since he himself gives to all men life and breath and everything. And he made from one every nation of men to live on all the face of the earth, having determined allotted periods and the boundaries of their habitation, that they should seek God, in the hope that they might feel after him and find him. Yet he is not far from each one of us, for

'In him we live and move and have our being';
as even some of your poets have said,

'For we are indeed his offspring.'

Being then God's offspring, we ought not to think that the Deity is like gold, or silver, or stone, a representation by the art and imagination of man. The times of ignorance God overlooked, but now he commands all men everywhere to repent, because he has fixed a day on which he will

judge the world in righteousness by a man whom he has appointed, and of this he has given assurance to all men by raising him from the dead."

(Acts 17:22-31)

Our Teacher and Saviour

"Truly, truly, I say to you, we speak of what we know, and bear witness to what we have seen; but you do not receive our testimony. If I have told you earthly things and you do not believe, how can you believe if I tell you heavenly things? No one has ascended into heaven but he who descended from heaven, the Son of man. And as Moses lifted up the serpent in the wilderness, so must the Son of man be lifted up, that whoever believes in him may have eternal life."

For God so loved the world that he gave his only Son, that whoever believes in him should not perish but have eternal life. For God sent the Son into the world, not to condemn the world, but that the world might be saved through him.

(Jn 3:11-17)

Reflection

To believe in Christ is not simply to accept the credal statement that Jesus, who was crucified under Pontius Pilate and rose from the dead, is the Son of God. Faith in Christ, like faith in God, involves the believer in a personal relationship with a living Lord, who is invisibly present, who knows all things through his Spirit, and who communicates wisdom and power to those who believe.

To have faith in Christ is to believe that he is God's Son who was sent into this world to be *our Teacher* (or, in the language of St John, he is the Son of Man who descended from heaven to reveal the Father); it is to believe that he died and rose again to be *our Saviour,* raised up

so that whosoever believes in him may have eternal life; it is to believe that he reigns at God's right hand as *Lord and Head of the Church;* and it is to believe that one day he will be *our Judge,* as St Paul announced to the Athenians.

All these titles of Christ—Teacher, Saviour, Lord, and Judge—describe the relationship in which Christ stands to us. Through faith we recognize and accept and welcome him as Teacher, Saviour, Lord and Judge. Our faith is not simply an intellectual assent to certain propositions about him. It is an act of submission, by which we enter into a personal relationship with him (and so with other believers). We entrust ourselves to him as a wise Teacher, wanting to be guided by his wisdom. We appeal to him as our Saviour, wanting him to grant us his divine forgiveness and cleanse our hearts by his Holy Spirit. We pray to him as Lord of the Church, wanting him to reveal his will to us and give us strength to do it. And we confess our responsibility to him as our future Judge.

One can have faith in a political or military leader, and accept him as teacher and guide. But faith in Christ establishes a far closer bond. St Paul could even say: 'I live, now not I, but Christ lives in me'—mysterious words! Just as the sun warms the earth and works in plants, making them grow, so Christ works mysteriously in us, making us grow into his likeness. Our desire, as faithful disciples of Christ, should be to become as like him as possible, by walking in the way of the beatitudes through the power of his Holy Spirit. Daily we are transformed into his likeness, from one degree of glory to another. At present this glory is hidden from us, as Christ's glory too is hidden with God; but the day of revelation will come.

Prayer

Come, Lord Jesus Christ, and live in us who believe in you, so that we may become like you, and others may recognize

you in us. Be with us to the end of our days, so that we need not fear your Judgment. Who livest and reignest with God the Father in the unity of the Holy Spirit, God, for ever and ever.

3

WHY BELIEVE IN CHRIST?

The Witness of the Spirit

O foolish Galatians! Who has bewitched you, before whose eyes Jesus Christ was publicly portrayed as crucified? Let me ask you only this: Did you receive the Spirit by works of the law, or by hearing with faith? Are you so foolish? Having begun with the Spirit, are you now ending with the flesh? Did you experience so many things in vain?—if it really is in vain. Does he who supplies the Spirit to you and works miracles among you do so by works of the law, or by hearing with faith?

(Gal 3:1-5)

The Witness of the Evangelist

Eight days later, the disciples were again in the house, and Thomas was with them. The doors were shut, but Jesus came and stood among them, and said, "Peace be with you." Then he said to Thomas, "Put your finger here, and see my hands; and put out your hand, and place it in my side; do not be faithless, but believing." Thomas answered him, "My Lord and my God!" Jesus said to him, "Have you believed because you have seen me? Blessed are those who have not seen and yet believe."

Now Jesus did many other signs in the presence of the disciples, which are not written in this book; but these are

written that you may believe that Jesus is the Christ, the Son of God, and that believing you may have life in his name.

(Jn 20:26-31)

Reflection

If a group of adult Christians set themselves to write down an answer to the question, 'Why do I continue to believe in Christ?', no doubt there would be a variety of answers. Some might say: 'I was brought up a Christian; I have never found any reason to abandon my faith: and I don't feel any inclination to abandon it—it makes sense.' This would be a fairly good answer, provided the person in question had thought about his faith, to assure himself that it did make sense.

But the two readings suggest that St Paul and St John would expect us to give rather different answers. St Paul would expect us to say: 'I know that through my faith I have experienced the power of the Spirit in my life. He is the seal upon my faith, testifying to its truth and validity!' And St John would expect us to say: 'I believe because I accept the witness of the apostles set before me by the evangelists.'

As a Christian grows older, he should try to weigh up the value of the witness of the evangelists. If one takes the trouble to study the gospels seriously, the centuries seem to fall away; one is in contact with the faith and preaching of the very earliest generation. St Paul and the evangelists write as men fully convinced of the truth of what they are saying, and one does not need to be an expert to recognize the value of their testimony. It suffices to be a 'good man and true', like an honest juryman.

But St John does not expect us to rely entirely on *his* witness. He assures us (in 7:16-17) that if we will take seriously the teaching of Jesus and try to do the will of God

as he explained it, we shall verify in our own experience that the teaching is divine wisdom, and the Teacher is one sent from God. In this way, the believer comes to rely less and less on the witness of the evangelist, and more and more on his own encounter with Christ through his words of instruction. St John illustrates this development in chapter 4: first of all, it is the witness of the Samaritan woman that brings the townspeople to Christ; but at the end of the chapter they say to her (v. 42): 'It is no longer because of your words that we believe, for we have heard for ourselves, and we know that this is indeed the Saviour of the world.'

When a man says he is losing faith in Christ, it is often because he is making no attempt to live by Christ's teaching. Conversely, the more seriously we try to live by the Sermon on the Mount, the stronger is the witness of the Spirit in our own lives. The Spirit bears witness to our spirit that the gospel is true.

Prayer

Grant, O heavenly Father, that as we strive to do your will, we may experience in our lives the witness of your Holy Spirit. Strengthen our faith; give us perseverance; and grant that each of us may win at least one new disciple for you before we die. Through Jesus Christ.

4

FAITH IN GOD AND FAITH IN CHRIST

Natural Revelation

The wrath of God is revealed from heaven against all ungodliness and wickedness of men who by their wickedness suppress the truth. For what can be known about God is plain to them, because God has shown it to them. Ever since the creation of the world his invisible nature, namely, his eternal power and deity, has been clearly perceived in the things that have been made. So they are without excuse; for although they knew God they did not honour him as God or give thanks to him, but they became futile in their thinking and their senseless minds were darkened. Claiming to be wise, they became fools, and exchanged the glory of the immortal God for images resembling mortal man or birds or animals or reptiles.

(Rom 1:18-23)

Supernatural Revelation

Then Jesus, deeply moved again, came to the tomb; it was a cave, and a stone lay upon it. Jesus said, "Take away the stone." Martha, the sister of the dead man, said to him, "Lord, by this time there will be an odour, for he has been dead four days." Jesus said to her, "Did I not tell you that if you would believe you would see the glory of God?" So they took away the stone. And Jesus lifted up his eyes and said, "Father, I thank thee that thou hast

heard me. I knew that thou hearest me always, but I have said this on account of the people standing by, that they may believe that thou didst send me." When he had said this, he cried with a loud voice, "Lazarus, come out." The dead man came out, his hands and feet bound with bandages, and his face wrapped with a cloth. Jesus said to them, "Unbind him, and let him go."

(Jn 11:38-44)

Reflection

According to Karl Barth, we cannot know God except through Christ; if we try to find our own way to the knowledge of God, apart from Christ, we shall never attain to the true God of the Bible. We may arrive at a philosophical God, conceived as the necessary being, but if we worship that kind of God, we shall be worshipping an idol. Natural theology leads to idolatry.

This may seem a very extreme view when we take into account what St Paul says in his Epistle to the Romans and in his speeches in Acts. He certainly seems to say that God reveals himself through nature, and that we can and ought to come to knowledge of him by reflection on this natural revelation. However, St Paul also says that although men *could* come to the knowledge of God through natural revelation, they failed to do so and fell away into idolatry. In St John chapter 5, Christ tells even the Jews of Jerusalem that they do not know God—they think they do, but they are mistaken, for if they knew God they would recognize his Son.

The narrative of the Raising of Lazarus shows how it is possible to come to belief in Christ and belief in God at one and the same time. A man must have some preconception of the meaning of the word 'God' but he need not yet believe in God when he reads the narrative of the Raising of Lazarus (or the resurrection of Jesus). If, having

read it, he decides to believe in Christ, he must at the same time believe in God whose Son Christ claims to be. Jesus first thanks his Father for giving him power to raise Lazarus, then calls him from the tomb. The miracle is the seal, guaranteeing at the same time both that Jesus is the Son of God, and that there is a God who acts in and through him. So it is possible for us to come to faith in God *through* faith in Christ.

That is what happens in the lives of most of us: we do not come to know God first by the use of our reason, then by reading the Old Testament, and finally by learning about Christ our Lord. Just the reverse! We learn of God through Christ, and in the light of what we have learned from him we study the Old Testament, and we attempt to construct a natural theology. While we are working out our natural theology, we are all the time guided by the teaching of Christ. In our knowledge of God and our faith in God, we are still very much disciples of Christ. There is much consolation in recognizing this.

Prayer

O Lord, God of mercy and compassion, make our hearts receptive of your revelation in nature, in the prophets, and in Jesus Christ our Lord; we give thanks for the gifts of knowledge which we have already received through him, and we beg you to make us able to communicate these gifts to others. Through the same Jesus Christ our Lord.

5

FAITH IS A GIFT

Transcendence and Humility

The Lord answered Job out of the whirlwind: "Who is this that darkens counsel by words without knowledge? Gird up your loins like a man, I will question you, and you shall declare to me.

"Where were you when I laid the foundation of the earth? Tell me, if you have understanding. Who determined its measurements—surely you know! Or who stretched the line upon it? On what were its bases sunk, or who laid its cornerstone, when the morning stars sang together, and all the sons of God shouted for joy?

"Or who shut in the sea with doors, when it burst forth from the womb; when I made clouds its garment, and thick darkness its swaddling band, and prescribed bounds for it, and set bars and doors, and said, 'Thus far shall you come, and no farther, and here shall your proud waves be stayed'?

Then Job answered the Lord: "Behold, I am of small account; what shall I answer thee? I lay my hand on my mouth. I have spoken once, and I will not answer; twice, but I will proceed no further." *(Job 38:1-11;40:3-5)*

Humility and Faith

As Jesus entered Capernaum, a centurion came forward to him, beseeching him and saying, "Lord, my servant is

lying paralyzed at home, in terrible distress." And he said to him, "I will come and heal him." But the centurion answered him, "Lord, I am not worthy to have you come under my roof; but only say the word, and my servant will be healed. For I am a man under authority, with soldiers under me; and I say to one, 'Go,' and he goes, and to another, 'Come,' and he comes, and to my slave, 'Do this,' and he does it." When Jesus heard him, he marvelled, and said to those who followed him, "Truly, I say to you, not even in Israel have I found such faith. I tell you, many will come from east and west and sit at table with Abraham, Isaac, and Jacob in the kingdom of heaven, while the sons of the kingdom will be thrown into the outer darkness; there men will weep and gnash their teeth." And to the centurion Jesus said, "Go; be it done for you as you have believed." And the servant was healed at that very moment.

(Mt 8:5-13)

Reflection

One of the mysterious things about faith is this: faith itself is a gift of God. If faith were our own personal contribution to the work of our salvation, we might claim to justify ourselves, since according to St Paul we are justified by faith. But from its very beginning, faith is the work of the Holy Spirit in us. It is not we who search for God and find him; he searches us out, even though we hide from him. If we meet him in faith, it is because he found us, and opened our hearts to listen to his revelation. No one comes to Christ unless he is drawn by the Father. In chapter 6 of St John, Jesus says to the Galileans (v.29): 'This is the work of God that you believe in him whom he has sent'—it is the work of God in two senses: the work which God requires us to do, and the work which he does in us, if we cooperate.

Another mysterious thing about faith is the uneven distribution of this gift. When St Paul preached at Athens,

the majority of his hearers turned away, but just a few believed—Dionysius the Areopagite, a woman named Damaris, and a few others (cf. Acts 17:34). Why these and not others? It is a mystery—the mystery of predestination. In the passage from St Matthew, Jesus himself marvels at the distribution of the gift of faith: the Gentile centurion shows greater faith than anyone in Israel! It was the same on Calvary—while the Jews mocked Christ, the centurion and his men were so impressed that they exclaimed: 'Truly this was the Son of God!' Pilate too made a wry confession of faith, when he wrote the title 'Jesus of Nazareth, King of the Jews' and refused to alter it.

God cares for all men, and wills the salvation of all. Yet only a minority believe in the cross of Christ! It is a mystery beyond our understanding. We must learn, however, from the Book of Job, not to question the justice of God simply because we cannot understand. His wisdom is infinitely greater than ours. What is required on our part is trust in his goodness and providence.

Since faith is a gift, we must always pray, like another father in the gospel: 'Lord, I believe; help thou my unbelief!' Give me a strong, charismatic belief, which will overflow into the lives of others. Give me a larger share in the fidelity of Christ your Son at the moment of his death, when he said: 'Father, into your hands I commend my spirit.'

Prayer

Heavenly Father, we believe that your power and wisdom are far beyond our understanding; strengthen our faith, so that we may trust you perfectly and live without fear. Grant that we may be strong enough to support the faith of others when they waver. Through Jesus Christ your Son our Lord.

6

REVELATION AS LIBERATION

The Freedom of Sons

Is the law against the promises of God? Certainly not; for if a law had been given which could make alive, then righteousness would indeed be by the law. But the scripture consigned all things to sin, that what was promised to faith in Jesus Christ might be given to those who believe.

Now before faith came, we were confined under the law, kept under restraint until faith should be revealed. So that the law was our custodian until Christ came, that we might be justified by faith. But now that faith has come, we are no longer under a custodian; for in Christ Jesus you are all sons of God, through faith.

(Gal 3:21-26)

Truth and Freedom

Jesus said to the Jews who had believed in him, "If you continue in my word, you are truly my disciples, and you will know the truth, and the truth will make you free." They answered him, "We are descendants of Abraham, and have never been in bondage to any one. How is it that you say, 'You will be made free'?"

Jesus answered them, "Truly, truly, I say to you, every one who commits sin is a slave to sin. The slave does

not continue in the house for ever; the Son continues for ever. So if the Son makes you free, you will be free indeed.
(*Jn 8:31-36*)

Reflection

Those who talk about revelation nowadays usually announce to us as a great discovery that revelation is not merely the communication of knowledge in the form of propositions; it is much more an encounter between persons. No doubt that is true in some sense of the word 'revelation'. But it seems to me much more important and much more scriptural to say: 'Revelation is not merely the communication of knowledge; it is the communication of *liberating* knowledge.' That point is made in both the readings: the truth revealed to us by Christ makes us free, says St John; it liberates us from the bondage of sin and from the bondage of the law, says St Paul.

St Paul's statements about liberation from the slavery of the law and from the curse of the law have always been offensive to Jews. They have always claimed, and still claim, that God made them free at the Exodus—he sent Moses to say to Pharaoh, 'Set my people free—that they may serve me.' Then at Sinai he explained how his people were to serve him in freedom. He describes himself at the beginning of the decalogue as the God of freedom: 'I am the Lord your God who brought you out of the land of Egypt and out of the house of bondage.' But Christ and St Paul both say to them: 'You are not free; freedom is to be obtained through *faith,* faith in Christ.'

Another point which is rarely made by writers on revelation and faith is that faith is not only our response to revelation, it is also the object of revelation. St Paul says: 'When *faith* was revealed we were set free...' In his view, the most liberating truth of all that is revealed in the gospel is that we are justified by *faith,* and not by works.

To Paul the Pharisee, this came as a great revelation and a great liberation: he no longer needed to try to make *himself* a just man; all he had to do was to believe in Christ and accept justification as a free gift. This revelation relieved him of the burden of trying to save his own soul by his own efforts alone.

The revelation of faith is that being associated through faith with Christ's perfect fidelity to God on the Cross, we are made sharers in his Holy Spirit. In revealing to us the efficacy of faith, God has revealed at the same time his own generous love: God so loved the world as to give his only Son. That is one sense in which revelation can be described as a personal encounter: in revealing the mystery of faith the Father reveals his own loving heart.

Prayer

Strengthen, O loving Father, the bond of faith uniting us to your Son, so that freed from every burden of ignorance, waywardness and guilt, we may walk easily along the path of salvation.

7

REVELATION AND SALVATION

Liberation from Egypt

On the third new moon after the people of Israel had gone forth out of the land of Egypt, on that day they came into the wilderness of Sinai. And when they set out from Rephidim and came into the wilderness of Sinai, they encamped in the wilderness; and there Israel encamped before the mountain. And Moses went up to God, and the Lord called to him out of the mountain, saying, "Thus you shall say to the house of Jacob, and tell the people of Israel: You have seen what I did to the Egyptians, and how I bore you on eagles' wings and brought you to myself. Now therefore, if you will obey my voice and keep my covenant, you shall be my own possession among all peoples; for all the earth is mine, and you shall be to me a kingdom of priests and a holy nation. These are the words which you shall speak to the children of Israel."

And God spoke all these words, saying, "I am the Lord your God, who brought you out of the land of Egypt, out of the house of bondage."

(Exod 19:1-6;20:1-2)

Liberation from Demons

Now Jesus was casting out a demon that was dumb; when the demon had gone out, the dumb man spoke, and the people marvelled. But some of them said, "He casts out

demons by Beelzebul, the prince of demons"; while others, to test him, sought from him a sign from heaven. But he, knowing their thoughts, said to them, "Every kingdom divided against itself is laid waste, and house falls upon house. And if Satan also is divided against himself, how will his kingdom stand? For you say that I cast out demons by Beelzebul. And if I cast out demons by Beelzebul, by whom do your sons cast them out? Therefore they shall be your judges. But if it is by the finger of God that I cast out demons, then the kingdom of God has come upon you. When a strong man, fully armed, guards his own palace, his goods are in peace; but when one stronger than he assails him and overcomes him, he takes away his armour in which he trusted, and divides his spoil. He who is not with me is against me, and he who does not gather with me scatters.

"When the unclean spirit has gone out of a man, he passes through waterless places seeking rest; and finding none he says, 'I will return to my house from which I came.' And when he comes he finds it swept and put in order. Then he goes and brings seven other spirits more evil than himself, and they enter and dwell there; and the last state of that man becomes worse than the first."

As he said this, a woman in the crowd raised her voice and said to him, "Blessed is the womb that bore you, and the breasts that you sucked!" But he said, "Blessed rather are those who hear the word of God and keep it!"

(Lk 11:14-28)

Reflection

At the beginning of this passage of the gospel, Jesus performs a notable miracle: he exorcises a dumb man, and the man begins to speak. It is a work of salvation, and at the same time a work of revelation. Jesus saves the unfortunate man from his disability, and at the same time he reveals his power to expel demons and to give more

abundant life. He reveals himself in action, but he acts primarily in order to save; he reveals himself as it were by the way, in saving the man.

It was the same at Sinai: God saved his people from the Egyptians, and in saving them he revealed himself: he showed them his concern for them and his desire to set them free—if they would accept his guidance and the leadership of Moses.

In the gospel passage, the scribes and Pharisees cannot deny the fact of the miraculous cure, but they can and do refuse to accept the revelation. Even a striking miracle is a revelation only to those who are *willing* to believe; goodwill is required on the part of the witnesses. Those who are well-disposed recognize in the exorcism the finger of God; those who are ill-disposed attribute it to the power of Satan. Everyone is challenged; no one can be neutral; those who say they 'don't know' are in fact rejecting the revelation.

Christ reasons with his opponents to make them feel ashamed of their obtuseness. But there are none so blind as those who do not wish to see. When Jesus performed an even greater miracle than this, they still refused to believe— for the trivial reason that the miracle had been worked on the sabbath, and work should not be done on this day. On that occasion too Christ reasoned with them, but they remained stubbornly incredulous.

As no one today is likely to attribute Christ's miracles to the power of Beelzebul, the first half of this gospel passage is only of antiquarian interest to us, as the record of an ancient controversy; but the second half is highly relevant. It tells us that so long as we have a lively faith and trust in Christ, we draw on his saving power, being inhabited by his Holy Spirit, and he will keep us free from the demons of pride, contentiousness, envy, lust, sloth and so on. But if our faith grows weak, the Holy Spirit withdraws and we become like an empty house, waiting for

demonic squatters — and we are warned that the last state may be worse than the first. Not all who begin well end well.

In a word, Christ is our Saviour, and we are safe as long as we cleave to him in faith and obedience.

Prayer

Reveal yourself to me, O Lord, in saving me from myself, so that having experienced your saving power, I may go out of myself and cleave to you.

8

FAITH IN MOSES AND FAITH IN CHRIST

The Diffidence of Moses

God also said to Moses, "Go and gather the elders of Israel together, and say to them, "The Lord, the God of your fathers, the God of Abraham, of Isaac, and of Jacob, has appeared to me, saying, "I have observed you and what has been done to you in Egypt; and I promise that I will bring you up out of the affliction of Egypt, to the land of the Canaanites, the Hittites, the Amorites, the Perizzites, the Hivites, and the Jebusites, a land flowing with milk and honey."

Then Moses answered, "But behold, they will not believe me or listen to my voice, for they will say, 'The Lord did not appear to you.'" The Lord said to him, "What is that in your hand?" He said, "A rod." And he said, "Cast it on the ground." So he cast it on the ground, and it became a serpent; and Moses fled from it. But the Lord said to Moses, "Put out your hand, and take it by the tail"—so he put out his hand and caught it, and it became a rod in his hand—"that they may believe that the Lord, the God of their fathers, the God of Abraham, the God of Isaac, and the God of Jacob, has appeared to you." Again, the Lord said to him, "Put your hand into your bosom." And he put his hand into his bosom; and when he took it out, behold, his hand was leprous, as white as snow. Then God said, "Put your hand back into your

bosom." So he put his hand back into his bosom; and when he took it out, behold, it was restored like the rest of his flesh. "If they will not believe you," God said, "or heed the first sign, they may believe the latter sign. If they will not believe even these two signs or heed your voice, you shall take some water from the Nile and pour it upon the dry ground; and the water which you shall take from the Nile will become blood upon the dry ground."

(Exod 3:16-17;4:1-9)

The Confidence of Christ

Again Jesus said to them, "I go away, and you will seek me and die in your sin; where I am going, you cannot come." Then said the Jews, "Will he kill himself, since he says, 'Where I am going, you cannot come'?" He said to them, "You are from below, I am from above; you are of this world, I am not of this world. I told you that you would die in your sins, for you will die in your sins unless you believe that I am he." They said to him, "Who are you?" Jesus said to them, "Even what I have told you from the beginning. I have much to say about you and much to judge; but he who sent me is true, and I declare to the world what I have heard from him." They did not understand that he spoke to them of the Father.

(Jn 8:21-27)

Reflection

The ancient Israelites were required to believe in Moses, and we are required to believe in Christ our Lord. There are similarities and there are differences.

The Israelites were to believe that Moses had been chosen by God to be his prophet or mouthpiece and to lead them out of Egypt into a land of their own; to commend Moses to their faith, God enabled him to perform certain miracles. Similarly Jesus was sent into the world to be

the mouthpiece of God and to open up the way into the kingdom of heaven; and to commend him to the faith of the Jews, God his Father enabled him to perform miracles.

But Moses never dared to forgive sins. He did not speak in his own person, but said: 'Thus saith the Lord.' Nor did he lay down his life for the salvation of his people, nor claim to be God's Son. But Jesus does claim to be God's Son—and he speaks and acts as God's Son. He forgives sins; and he says 'Amen, Amen, I say to you'; and he lays down his life as a ransom for the many who believe in him.

So, while the Jew of today looks back to Moses as a prophet and a teacher whose influence continues through the books attributed to him and through the congregation which under God he founded, the Christian of today looks to Christ as still living and reigning with his Father and acting through his ministers in the Church. Moses raised up the Brazen Serpent in the desert, which was a type of Jesus who was to come; it is he, and not Moses, who offers forgiveness and peace both to the believing Jew and to the believing Gentile.

Prayer

We believe, Lord Jesus, that you are our guide, travelling with us through the world towards the Promised Land; in your Body dwells the Shekinah; in you is the source of forgiveness, and in you are the fountains of wisdom and knowledge.

9

GOD IS REVEALED AS A GOD OF PEACE

Commotion at Sinai

At Horeb [1] Elijah came to a cave, and lodged there; and behold, the word of the Lord came to him, and he said to him, "What are you doing here, Elijah?" He said, "I have been very jealous for the Lord, the God of hosts; for the people of Israel have forsaken thy covenant, thrown down thy altars, and slain thy prophets with the sword; and I, even I only, am left; and they seek my life, to take it away." And he said, "Go forth, and stand upon the mount before the Lord." And behold, the Lord passed by, and a great and strong wind rent the mountains, and broke in pieces the rocks before the Lord, but the Lord was not in the wind; and after the wind an earthquake, but the Lord was not in the earthquake; and after the earthquake a fire, but the Lord was not in the fire; and after the fire a still small voice.

(1 Kgs 19:9-12)

Commotion at Pentecost

When the day of Pentecost had come, they were all together in one place. And suddenly a sound came from heaven like the rush of a mighty wind, and it filled all the house where they were sitting. And there appeared to them tongues as of fire, distributed and resting on each one of them. And

---

[1] 'Horeb' is another name for Sinai

they were all filled with the Holy Spirit and began to speak in other tongues, as the Spirit gave them utterance.

Now there were dwelling in Jerusalem Jews, devout men from every nation under heaven. And at this sound the multitude came together, and they were bewildered, because each one heard them speaking in his own language. And they were amazed and wondered, saying, "Are not all these who are speaking Galileans? And how is it that we hear, each of us in his own native language? Parthians and Medes and Elamites and residents of Mesopotamia, Judea and Cappadocia, Pontus and Asia, Phrygia and Pamphylia, Egypt and the parts of Libya belonging to Cyrene, and visitors from Rome, both Jews and proselytes, Cretans and Arabians, we hear them telling in our own tongues the mighty works of God."

(Acts 2:1-11)

The Quiet Paraclete

Jesus answered "If a man loves me, he will keep my word, and my Father will love him, and we will come to him and make our home with him. He who does not love me does not keep my words; and the word which you hear is not mine but the Father's who sent me.

"These things I have spoken to you, while I am still with you. But the Counsellor, the Holy Spirit, whom the Father will send in my name, he will teach you all things, and bring to your remembrance all that I have said to you. Peace I leave with you; my peace I give to you; not as the world gives do I give to you. Let not your hearts be troubled, neither let them be afraid."

(Jn 14:23-27)

Reflection

As we listen to the account of the first pentecostal outpouring of the Spirit, no doubt we all think to our-

selves: 'What a pity such things don't happen today! How much more interesting and exciting our religious life would be, if the Holy Spirit settled upon each of us like a tongue of fire, and enabled us to talk in strange languages!' But such things don't happen to us.

It was the same in Old Testament times—the Jews continually looked back to their beginnings, to the great manifestations of divine power at the Exodus and at Mt Sinai, hoping for a repetition—which never came. Elijah actually went back to Sinai in the Arabian desert and God granted him a vision there—a whirlwind, an earthquake, and a fire—all the externals of the Sinai-theophany: but he was taught that God was not in the whirlwind, and God was not in the earthquake, and God was not in the fire—but in the still small voice of conscience within him. He is a God of peace, not of commotion; we should not expect him to create a commotion at his coming.

So then, if we look back longingly to the morning of Pentecost, wishing for a display of extraordinary charismata, perhaps we are making the mistake of Elijah. God does not repeat the foundation miracles which he performed to get the Church off the ground. He is still present, but in a different way, as St John says in this passage from the gospel: If any man loves him, keeps his commandments, obeys the still small voice within, then he and the Father will come and lodge securely within him. That is what *we* should hope and pray for: the secret indwelling of the Son and the Father through their Holy Spirit, creating peace.

Prayer

Come, O Holy Spirit, and fill our hearts with the peace of Christ which passes all understanding, so that we may discern the will of God our Father, and love it, and do it.

10

THE STAGES OF REVELATION

Revelation to Paul

Paul said, "As I made my journey and drew near to Damascus, about noon a great light from heaven suddenly shone about me. And I fell to the ground and heard a voice saying to me. 'Saul, Saul, why do you persecute me?' And I answered, 'Who are you, Lord?' And he said to me, 'I am Jesus of Nazareth whom you are persecuting.' Now those who were with me saw the light but did not hear the voice of the one who was speaking to me. And I said, 'What shall I do, Lord?' And the Lord said to me, 'Rise, and go into Damascus, and there you will be told all that is appointed for you to do.' And when I could not see because of the brightness of that light, I was led by the hand by those who were with me, and came into Damascus.

"And one Ananias, a devout man according to the law, well spoken of by all the Jews who lived there, came to me, and standing by me said to me, 'Brother Saul, receive your sight.' And in that very hour I received my sight and saw him. And he said, 'The God of our fathers appointed you to know his will, to see the Just One and to hear a voice from his mouth; for you will be a witness for him to all men of what you have seen and heard. And now why do you wait? Rise and be baptized, and wash away your sins, calling on his name.'

"When I had returned to Jerusalem and was praying in the temple, I fell into a trance and saw him saying to me, 'Make haste and get quickly out of Jerusalem, because they will not accept your testimony about me.' And I said, 'Lord, they themselves know that in every synagogue I imprisoned and beat those who believed in thee. And when the blood of Stephen thy witness was shed, I also was standing by and approving, and keeping the garments of those who killed him.' And he said to me, 'Depart; for I will send you far away to the Gentiles.'"

(Acts 22:6-21)

Revelation to the Disciples

At that time Jesus declared, "I thank thee, Father, Lord of heaven and earth, that thou hast hidden these things from the wise and understanding and revealed them to babes; yea, Father, for such was thy gracious will. All things have been delivered to me by my Father; and no one knows the Son except the Father, and no one knows the Father except the Son and any one to whom the Son chooses to reveal him. Come to me, all who labour and are heavy laden, and I will give you rest. Take my yoke upon you, and learn from me; for I am gentle and lowly in heart, and you will find rest for your souls. For my yoke is easy, and my burden is light."

(Mt 11:25-30)

Reflection

As this passage of the gospel is loosely attached to its context in St Matthew and occurs in quite a different context in St Luke, we are left to guess on what occasion Jesus actually said the words recorded in it. Perhaps a likely guess would be that Jesus said these things just after the Transfiguration: he thanks his Father that the disciples have been given this revelation, and calls upon

all to accept the yoke of his teaching—just as the voice from heaven in the Transfiguration says: 'Hear ye him!'

St Paul's vision on the road to Damascus and the Transfiguration were moments of revelation in the lives of the four greatest apostles, Peter and Paul and John and James. There is revelation-in-act (God acts in each case to reveal the glory of his Son), and there is revelation-in-word (the words spoken give the meaning of the two visions: 'This is my beloved Son,' and 'I am Jesus whom you are persecuting'). In the Bible, revelation-in-act constantly goes together with revelation-in-word.

Neither the Transfiguration nor St Paul's Damascus-vision was complete in itself. Through these preliminary experiences, the disciples were being made ready for their task as preachers of the gospel. Revelation is not complete until the good news of God's action for our salvation is made known by the apostles to their hearers (cf. Acts 2:37). The 'deposit' of revelation was complete at the end of the apostolic age; but the process of revelation is never complete; it goes on and on as the gospel is preached to each new generation and believed by more and more men. The life, death and resurrection of Christ may be compared to a radio mast constantly transmitting a message from God; revelation or communication takes place where and when the message is received.

Therefore revelation should not be thought of as something which happened long ago, two thousand years before we were born. It continues in our midst and in our own lives, as we believe and receive the impulses of the Holy Spirit. Christ reveals himself and his Father to those whom he chooses in each generation; and he chooses the little ones. If we are really wise, then, we will humble ourselves in his presence and make no pretence of being 'wise and prudent'. Then perhaps he will open our minds to understand the scriptures, and still more to grasp the events narrated in the scriptures. Unless he choose to reveal

himself, we shall look and look yet never see; we shall hear and hear, yet never understand.

Prayer

Open the eyes of our minds, O heavenly Father, to receive the light of your revelation, as we contemplate the life, death and resurrection of your Son in the pages of the holy books left to us by your prophets and apostles.

11

MOMENTS OF REVELATION

A Painful Revelation

Peter said, "Men of Israel, hear these words: Jesus of Nazareth, a man attested to you by God with mighty works and wonders and signs which God did through him in your midst, as you yourselves know—this Jesus, delivered up according to the definite plan and foreknowledge of God, you crucified and killed by the hands of lawless men. But God raised him up, having loosed the pangs of death, because it was not possible for him to be held by it. For David says concerning him, 'I saw the Lord always before me, for he is at my right hand that I may not be shaken; therefore my heart was glad, and my tongue rejoiced; moreover my flesh will dwell in hope. For thou wilt not abandon my soul to Hades, nor let thy Holy One see corruption. Thou hast made known to me the ways of life; thou wilt make me full of gladness with thy presence.'

"Brethren, I may say to you confidently of the patriarch David that he both died and was buried, and his tomb is with us to this day. Being therefore a prophet, and knowing that God had sworn with an oath to him that he would set one of his descendants upon his throne, he foresaw and spoke of the resurrection of the Christ, that he was not abandoned to Hades, nor did his flesh see corruption. This Jesus God raised up, and of that we all are witnesses. Being therefore exalted at the right hand of God, and having received from the Father the promise of the Holy

Spirit, he has poured out this which you see and hear. For David did not ascend into the heavens; but he himself says, 'The Lord said to my Lord, Sit at my right hand, till I make thy enemies a stool for thy feet.'

Let all the house of Israel therefore know assuredly that God has made him both Lord and Christ, this Jesus whom you crucified."

Now when they heard this they were cut to the heart, and said to Peter and the rest of the apostles, "Brethren, what shall we do?"

(Acts 2:22-37)

An Awesome Revelation

Behold, the curtain of the temple was torn in two, from top to bottom; and the earth shook, and the rocks were split; the tombs also were opened, and many bodies of the saints who had fallen asleep were raised, and coming out of the tombs after his resurrection they went into the holy city and appeared to many. When the centurion and those who were with him, keeping watch over Jesus, saw the earthquake and what took place, they were filled with awe, and said, "Truly this was the Son of God!"

(Mt 27:51-54)

Reflection

In ordinary speech, if anyone says: 'It was an absolute revelation to me,' he means that he was suddenly hit by some surprising new insight, which caused excitement and delight—or perhaps dismay. Scientists sometimes talk of having a sudden 'inspiration' or of receiving a blinding flash of 'revelation.' The Transfiguration was such a moment in the lives of Peter, James and John—they were suddenly surprised and delighted. Again, the resurrection appearance of Jesus to Thomas was a moment of astonishment and adoration, as his mind yielded and he accepted the truth of the resurrection—a truth which at first all the disciples had found too good to be true (cf Lk 24:41).

The two readings describe moments of revelation of a less happy sort: the preaching of Peter enabled the Jews to recognise with horror that they had crucified the Messiah, and they were cut to the quick. And in the gospel reading, the manner of Jesus' death revealed to the Roman soldiers that it was indeed God's Son whom they had put to death.

For us who have been Christians all our lives, the Cross may have ceased to be a scandal, through sheer familiarity; and the resurrection may no longer stir any emotional response. The word 'revelation' in religious contexts can lose its emotional overtones and become a bit of theological jargon.

And yet it is to be hoped that there will be moments of revelation in the life of every Christian. A glorious sunset at sea, or some deeply moving personal experience, may suddenly fill the mind with wonder at the splendour of creation and the goodness of its Maker; and it is to be hoped that there will be moments during the liturgy, or in time of retreat, when the words of a preacher, or the crucifix contemplated with faith, will become a greater revelation of the lovingkindness of God than any sunset could be.

Moments of revelation do not come to a scientist unless he has prepared his mind by patient seeking. Perhaps the same is true of seekers after God: the goodness of the Good News does not strike us until we have prepared our minds by recollection, reflection, and petition for enlightenment.

Prayer

Renew in me, O Lord, the heart of a child, so that the joy of the gospel may once again fill my heart to overflowing, and thrill my mind with wonder, as in the days of my childhood, when I knelt beside a crib at Christmas.

12

REVEALED TRUTHS
NATURAL AND SUPERNATURAL

Revelation and the Well-Ordered Life

The grace of God has appeared for the salvation of all men, training us to renounce irreligion and worldly passions, and to live sober, upright, and godly lives in this world, awaiting our blessed hope, the appearing of the glory of our great God and Saviour Jesus Christ, who gave himself for us to redeem us from all iniquity and to purify for himself a people of his own who are zealous for good deeds.

(Tit 2:11-14)

The Principle of Good Order

"You have heard that it was said, 'You shall love your neighbour and hate your enemy.' But I say to you, Love your enemies and pray for those who persecute you, so that you may be sons of your Father who is in heaven; for he makes his sun rise on the evil and on the good, and sends rain on the just and on the unjust. For if you love those who love you, what reward have you? Do not even the tax collectors do the same? And if you salute only your brethren, what more are you doing than others? Do not even the Gentiles do the same? You, therefore, must be perfect, as your heavenly Father is perfect."

(Mt 5:43-48)

Reflection

The Muslim theologians have an interesting argument to show the *probability* of revelation, that is, to show that God being what he is, and man being what he is, it is likely that God will reveal his will to men. By nature, they argue, man is a gregarious animal. He cannot live in isolation; if he were not taught a language by other men, his thought processes would be so elementary that he would hardly be human. But unlike bees and ants, men do not know instinctively how to live together in peace and harmony. Is it not probable then, they ask, that God in his goodness will raise up among men a few who are specially gifted, and then grant them special graces of insight, so that they will see and promulgate the rules necessary for the peaceful ordering of human life?

This line of argument has its attractions, but it leads to the question: What *was* the gift of prophecy possessed by the Old Testament prophets —and by John the Baptist, and by Christ, who was a prophet and much more than a prophet? Is a prophet simply one whose natural powers are enhanced by God's grace to discern what was there all the time waiting to be seen? Many of the utterances of the prophets on social matters can certainly be accounted for in this way. Amos needed no vision to tell him that it was sinful to sell the righteous for silver, and the needy for a pair of shoes (cf Amos 2:6); Isaiah could see for himself the sinfulness of pampered women whose extravagance drove their husbands to extortion (cf Isa 3: 16ff); John the Baptist hardly needed an angelic visitor to tell him that he who has two coats should give to him that has none (cf Lk 3:11); and the same can be said of many parts of the Sermon on the Mount: Jesus did not need to learn these things by receiving preternatural infused knowledge. The natural powers of discernment of his human mind, aided by divine grace, could recognise the shortcomings of the law and the Pharisaic tradition, and could

fulfil what was wanting. In part, supernatural revelation is simply the natural revelation recognised and expressed with the aid of supernatural grace. The Wisdom literature contains 'revelation' of this kind.

However, there were other truths revealed by Christ which he cannot have learned in this way—about future judgment, about the rebirth of man in baptism, and about the timetable of his own ministry. Nathanael was told that he would see angels ascending and descending over the Son of Man (Jn 1:51)—by which Jesus meant that Nathanael would recognise that he was in constant communication with the Father. The mind of Christ was on the horizon of the two worlds; he revealed to us mysteries which human reason could never have discovered—about his own relation to the Father, about our baptism in the Spirit, about our future judgment and future glory. A disciple is not greater than his master: if the master has eyes the disciple can see. Christ has the eyes of more than a prophet; he sees far beyond our horizon.

Prayer

Teach us, Lord Jesus, how we should live in this world, and how we should prepare for future Judgment; for these things are known to you as no other man has known them, and you alone have power to penetrate our minds, to free us from dangerous error.

13

FAITH DRIVES OUT FEAR

Fear of Death

It was fitting that he, for whom and by whom all things exist, in bringing many sons to glory, should make the pioneer of their salvation perfect through suffering. For he who sanctifies and those who are sanctified have all one origin. That is why he is not ashamed to call them brethren, saying, "I will proclaim thy name to my brethren, in the midst of the congregation I will praise thee." And again, "I will put my trust in him." And again, "Here am I, and the children God has given me."

Since therefore the children share in flesh and blood, he himself likewise partook of the same nature, that through death he might destroy him who has the power of death, that is, the devil, and deliver all those who through fear of death were subject to lifelong bondage.

(Heb 2:10-15)

Fear drives out Faith

When Jesus got into the boat, his disciples followed him. And behold, there arose a great storm on the sea, so that the boat was being swamped by the waves; but he was asleep. And they went and woke him, saying, "Save, Lord; we are perishing." And he said to them, "Why are you afraid, O men of little faith?" Then he rose and rebuked

the winds and the sea; and there was a great calm. And the men marvelled, saying, "What sort of man is this, that even winds and sea obey him?"

(Mt 8:23-27)

Reflection

The closing verse of the passage from Hebrews presents a problem: Is it true that people who have not heard or believed the gospel 'are subject to lifelong bondage through fear of death'? Nowadays the literature of Humanists shows little sign of any such bondage. Most people seem to put death out of mind as successfully as they forget about atomic war. Is it true, then, that faith in the gospel drives out fear of death?

Perhaps in the ancient world things were different. The causes of diseases were unknown, and there was little protection—one could easily die of appendicitis. The Roman poet Lucretius says something very much like the passage from Hebrews: that 'everything is smeared with the blackness of death.' Perhaps we don't realize how much our faith has done for us in this respect. If we believed that after death we are to drag on an endless, colourless, loveless existence in Sheol, and therefore that every hope we have of enjoying good things is entirely in this life, no doubt we should have a much greater dread of death. The Christian faith has exorcised this dread by assuring us that the next life will be better than this—that death will not be a loss of life but a positive gain.

Therefore we should be able to face death, particularly in old age, without fear, and with positive *hope*, believing that what lies beyond death will be better than the burden of living on in old age.

In the gospel passage, the disciples fear death by drowning, and Christ reproaches them. We are always in his hand, whether we live or whether we die. We must preserve

our souls in peace, as a proof of our faith in him. Faith should create peace; justified by faith, we are at peace with God, and being at peace with him now, we look forward to seeing his glory hereafter.

Prayer

Grant, O Lord, that when in old age we are tired of living, we may not be afraid of dying; for you have drawn the sting of death.

14

THE CERTAINTY OF FAITH

The Strength of Moses

By faith Moses, when he was grown up, refused to be called the son of Pharaoh's daughter, choosing rather to share ill-treatment with the people of God than to enjoy the fleeting pleasures of sin. He considered abuse suffered for the Christ greater wealth than the treasures of Egypt, for he looked to the reward. By faith he left Egypt, not being afraid of the anger of the king; for he endured as seeing him who is invisible.

(Heb 11:24-27)

The Strong and the Weak

Those who had seized Jesus led him to Caiaphas the high priest, where the scribes and the elders had gathered. But Peter followed him at a distance, as far as the courtyard of the high priest, and going inside he sat with the guards to see the end. Now the chief priests and the whole council sought false testimony against Jesus that they might put him to death, but they found none, though many false witnesses came forward. At last two came forward and said, "This fellow said, 'I am able to destroy the temple of God, and to build it in three days.'" And the high priest stood up and said, "Have you no answer to make? What is it that these men testify against you?" But Jesus was silent. And the high priest said to him, "I adjure you by the living

God, tell us if you are the Christ, the Son of God." Jesus said to him, "You have said so. But I tell you, hereafter you will see the Son of man seated at the right hand of Power, and coming on the clouds of heaven." Then the high priest tore his robes, and said, "He has uttered blasphemy. Why do we still need witnesses? You have now heard his blasphemy. What is your judgment?" They answered, "He deserves death." Then they spat in his face, and struck him; and some slapped him, saying, "Prophesy to us, you Christ! Who is it that struck you?"

Now Peter was sitting outside in the courtyard. And a maid came up to him, and said, "You also were with Jesus the Galilean." But he denied it before them all, saying, "I do not know what you mean."

(Mt 26:57-70)

Reflection

At the beginning of chapter 11 of the Epistle to the Hebrews, faith is described as 'conviction of things not seen.' Later in the same chapter the author gives us the fine example of Moses: he showed his faith when he left Egypt without fearing the anger of the king. He had before his eyes the anger of the Pharaoh, but he had greater respect for the invisible King of heaven. There we see in a vivid human situation just what religious faith means, how it can be a source of manly strength, and how admirable it is in its effects. Moses sees before his bodily eyes the wrath of Pharaoh, but with the eyes of his soul he sees the majesty of God, in comparison with which the power of Pharaoh is nothing. Faith, by driving out fear, is a secret source of strength, which commands admiration.

Moses is a 'type', prefiguring Christ. Moses was faithful as a servant is faithful in a household not his own; Jesus was faithful as a Son in his Father's house. Just as Moses feared at first to undertake the leadership of his people,

so Christ too struggled against his commission, in Gethsemane. But when he confronted his judges—the Jewish court under Caiaphas and later the Roman governor, Pilate—he showed no sign of fear, but maintained an impressive calm, at which Pilate marvelled. And on Calvary the Roman soldiers were convinced by his behaviour that he was indeed God's Son. The secret spring of his strength and courage was his fidelity to his Father. He was superior to fear because he had greater reverence for his Father whom he could not see, than for his judges who were there before his eyes. This fidelity was like a secret lifeline to his Father, a Jacob's ladder on which his thoughts ascended and descended.

At the beginning of the Acts of the Apostles (4:19-20), when Caiaphas forbids Peter and John to preach in the name of Jesus, they reply: 'Whether it is right in the sight of God to listen to you rather than to God, you must judge; for we cannot but speak of what we have seen and heard.' They too have become men of faith.

The same is required of all believers. We must maintain a secret channel of communication with God, and give him our first allegiance. In this way he will give us the strength to resist the power of fear and of lust. Men will see our good works, and give glory to our Father in heaven.

Prayer

Strengthen, O Lord, our conviction of the reality of things not seen, lest we spend all our time and energy over what we shall eat and what we shall drink and what we shall put on. Teach us, day by day, to trust in your loving Providence; and bring us safely to the Promised Land.

15

A COVENANT STRONGER THAN DEATH

Death Vanquished

Lo! I tell you a mystery. We shall not all sleep, but we shall all be changed, in a moment, in the twinkling of an eye, at the last trumpet. For the trumpet will sound, and the dead will be raised imperishable, and we shall be changed. For this perishable nature must put on the imperishable, and this mortal nature must put on immortality. When the perishable puts on the imperishable, and the mortal puts on immortality, then shall come to pass the saying that is written: "Death is swallowed up in victory." "O death, where is thy victory? O death, where is thy sting?" The sting of death is sin, and the power of sin is the law. But thanks be to God, who gives us the victory through our Lord Jesus Christ.

Therefore, my beloved brethren, be steadfast, immovable, always abounding in the work of the Lord, knowing that in the Lord your labour is not in vain.

(1 Cor 15:51-58)

Why we are Safe

Jesus said to the Jews, "I am the bread of life; he who comes to me shall not hunger, and he who believes in me shall never thirst. But I said to you that you have seen me and yet do not believe. All that the Father gives me will come to me; and him who comes to me I will not cast out. For I have come down from heaven, not to do my own

will, but the will of him who sent me; and this is the will of him who sent me, that I should lose nothing of all that he has given me, but raise it up at the last day. For this is the will of my Father, that every one who sees the Son and believes in him should have eternal life; and I will raise him up at the last day."

(Jn 6:35-40)

Reflection

We claim that a Christian enjoys 'certainty' in his faith. 'Certainty' is a cheerful word. It implies, on the one hand, strength, assurance and confidence in God; and on the other hand, immunity from error and deception. Thanks to Christ's revelation, a Christian knows where he has come from and where he is going. He is at peace, because God is with him. God has taken him into a covenant or partnership, and has imparted to him a share in his own fidelity.

In a human covenant or partnership, there can never be perfect certainty—not even in marriage. Every human being is frail, may change for the worse, may forget or renounce his promises, may act foolishly, or misunderstand. And every human covenant comes to an end—even marriage, which rests on a promise 'till death do us part.' But in a covenant with God, there is room for perfect certainty and unqualified, unlimited trust, because God is wise, good and just. When the Bible describes him as 'just', it usually means that he is faithful to his covenant promises. A Christian's faith *ought* to be perfectly certain, because in the one whom he is trusting there is perfect fidelity. The certainty of our faith rests on the rock-like fidelity of God —the rock of ages. And our covenant with him is not limited by death; on the contrary, it will be transformed and brought to its perfection at death.

In the marriage ceremony, a bride and bridegroom pledge fidelity and loyalty to each other for life. If they are good people and already know each other well, they

may place complete trust in each other. They may feel certain of each other's love and loyalty. But a bystander in the ceremony may sadly reflect that if sorely tempted, say through long separation, their fidelity might crack. With frail human beings complete certainty is not possible.

In the covenant between Christ and his Church, there can be and is complete certainty, because Christ does not change—he is the same yesterday, today and tomorrow (cf Heb 13:8); those who come to him he will never cast out (Jn 6:37)—his love is stronger than death and will rescue them out of death into his kingdom; he does not go back on his invitation or repent of his gifts of grace (cf Rom 11:29). The human members of the covenant with Christ have, therefore, objectively the most complete certainty in Christ. But they must make it their own by *willing* to trust completely in the fidelity of Christ and entrusting themselves without reserve to his guidance.

This comparison with marriage breaks down in so far as Christ is the *absent* bridegroom, who deliberately tests the fidelity of his spouse. Because he is out of sight, there is a danger of our forgetting him and quietly renouncing our fidelity. Therefore, if a Christian considers himself, he cannot feel entirely secure: he will wonder about his own perseverance. But that is just what he must *not* do. He must not consider himself—that was the mistake of St Peter as he walked on the water. We must look to Christ, and trust in his saving power, and believe that with every test he will provide the outcome (cf. 1 Cor 10:13). So long as we do this, we shall be perfectly secure.

Prayer

Look not, O heavenly Father, upon our frailties and infidelities, but on the faith of Jesus Christ your Son; let his strength make up for our weakness and bring us safely through the perils of this life and through the night of death into the light of your kingdom.

16

FAITH AND HONOUR

The Forbearance of God

No man has power to retain the spirit, or authority over the day of death; there is no discharge from war, nor will wickedness deliver those who are given to it. All this I observed while applying my mind to all that is done under the sun, while man lords it over man to his hurt.

Then I saw the wicked buried; they used to go in and out of the holy place, and were praised in the city where they had done such things. This also is vanity. Because sentence against an evil deed is not executed speedily, the heart of the sons of men is fully set to do evil. Though a sinner does evil a hundred times and prolongs his life, yet I know that it will be well with those who fear God, because they fear before him; but it will not be well with the wicked, neither will he prolong his days like a shadow, because he does not fear before God.

There is a vanity which takes place on earth, that there are righteous men to whom it happens according to the deeds of the wicked, and there are wicked men to whom it happens according to the deeds of the righteous. I said that this also is vanity. And I commend enjoyment, for man has no good thing under the sun but to eat, and drink, and enjoy himself, for this will go with him in his toil through the days of life which God gives him under the sun. *(Eccles 8:8-15)*

Two Types of Servant

"Who is the faithful and wise servant, whom his master has set over his household, to give them their food at the proper time? Blessed is that servant whom his master when he comes will find so doing. Truly, I say to you, he will set him over all his possessions. But if that wicked servant says to himself, 'My master is delayed,' and begins to beat his fellow servants, and eats and drinks with the drunken, the master of that servant will come on a day when he does not expect him and at an hour he does not know, and will punish him, and put him with the hypocrites; there men will weep and gnash their teeth."

(Mt 24:45-51)

Reflection

Christ's parable describes the situation of every believer during this life. He is like a servant who has been entrusted with some charge by his absent master; he is in a position of trust, and his fidelity is put to the test of time. He is placed on his honour, and is responsible: when the Lord returns, he must respond to all questions and render his accounts.

The lesson is specially applicable to those who have received some authority over their fellow-men, or some ministry to fulfil: anyone who has lorded it over his fellow-men to their hurt, will have to answer for his conduct. But every Christian is on his honour—to obey his conscience as formed by Christ's teaching in the gospels. He must not tell himself that Judgment is far away, that the Lord seems to take no notice, that he can get away with a few liberties and an occasional indiscretion. He is being left alone to prove his worth by acting responsibly and fulfilling his obligations. When one goes into a hospital at two o'clock in the morning, it is wonderful to see the nurses going quietly and peacefully about their jobs, as if

it were mid-day. The Christian life should be like that: we are always on duty.

As the passage from Ecclesiastes says, when the sinner finds that his sin is not immediately punished, he loses his respect for his conscience, and his heart is fully set to do evil; and the just man, when he sees the impunity of the wicked, may wonder whether, after all, God cares. That is the temptation to which Ecclesiastes seems to succumb. But the Christian must reaffirm his belief that God is just and does care. His forbearance is for our good— to give the just an opportunity to prove their worth by perseverance, and to give the sinners an opportunity to repent, seek forgiveness and make amends, before the day comes when he will demand a reckoning.

As St Paul observed, it is easy to misunderstand the forbearance of God (cf Rom 3:26). God has made us free, and leaves us to use our freedom. He wants us to serve him freely, loyally and responsibly, like adult sons; he does not force us to obey him like reluctant schoolboys.

We must, therefore, reverence our own conscience, through which our absent Lord speaks to us. We must not weaken it by disobeying it and treating it with contempt. We must pray for Christ's Holy Spirit to quicken it and make it a better mouthpiece of the will of God, so that when Christ judges us he will find us guilty neither of transgressions, nor of serious omissions. If those rejected at the judgment scene in Mt 25 had had a tender conscience, they would not have said: 'Lord, when did we see you hungry?'

Prayer

Quicken our consciences, O Lord, so that we may not be deaf to your will; give us courage and patience to persevere in loyal service, remembering that your unseen presence is always with us.

17

THE DISCIPLE AND HIS MASTER

What Paul professes to teach

Among the mature we do impart wisdom, although it is not a wisdom of this age or of the rulers of this age, who are doomed to pass away. But we impart a secret and hidden wisdom of God, which God decreed before the ages for our glorification. None of the rulers of this age understood this; for if they had, they would not have crucified the Lord of glory. But, as it is written, "What no eye has seen, nor ear heard, nor the heart of man conceived, what God has prepared for those who love him," God has revealed to us through the Spirit. For the Spirit searches everything, even the depths of God. For what person knows a man's thoughts except the spirit of the man which is in him? So also no one comprehends the thoughts of God except the Spirit of God. Now we have received not the spirit of the world, but the Spirit which is from God, that we might understand the gifts bestowed on us by God. And we impart this in words not taught by human wisdom but taught by the Spirit, interpreting spiritual truths to those who possess the Spirit.

(1 Cor 2:6-13)

What Jesus offers his Disciples

"All things have been delivered to me by my Father; and no one knows the Son except the Father; and no one knows the Father except the Son and any one to whom the Son chooses to reveal him. Come to me, all who labour

and are heavy laden, and I will give you rest. Take my yoke upon you, and learn from me; for I am gentle and lowly in heart, and you will find rest for your souls. For my yoke is easy, and my burden is light."

(Mt 11:27-30)

Reflection

The relationship between a student and his teacher should be one of mutual faith. If the student does not put faith in his teacher, he will not be a receptive disciple. He must believe that the teacher has something valuable to teach him, that he knows what he is talking about, that he is willing to communicate ungrudgingly what he knows, and that he will not teach errors.

In Greek, the word for 'professing' is identical with the word for 'promising.' The teacher professes to be able to impart to the student a body of knowledge or a certain skill—the law of contract, or how to remove an appendix, or how to speak a foreign language. The teacher begins by making a promise, and the disciple accepts it. The relationship implies that the disciple makes an act of faith in his teacher; he believes him to be a man of integrity who *can* do what he professes to be able to do, and that he will do so. In ancient Greece, where university education first began, the disciple promised to pay personally a certain sum of money to the teacher. Now that teaching is institutionalised, the point has been obscured, but of its nature the teacher-disciple relationship is a covenant between two persons, bound to each other in fidelity, and progressively in gratitude too.

In the passage from Mt 11, Jesus professes and promises. He offers himself as a Teacher, professing to know God and the will of God, inviting men to come and learn from him, and promising that if they do, they will find rest for their souls. The response which he asks for is first faith, then obedience. St Peter, at the end of the Galilean narrative of St John, exemplifies the faith required

in a disciple: 'Lord, to whom shall we go? You have the words of eternal life' (Jn 6:68). Peter and the other disciples did not yet understand Christ's teaching, any more than the other Galileans did, but they trusted him and were willing to go on following him in the conviction that he would teach them what they wanted to know—the words of eternal life, or how a man must live in order to enter the kingdom of God. They had seen his glory at Cana and in later miracles, and were therefore ready to believe his word even before they heard it. Here we see what is meant by saying that faith is a personal relationship: it is willingness to believe what a person says because he is who he is.

Many a human teacher does not live up to his profession: the course he gives disappoints the students and does not give them the ability they hoped to acquire. But Christ cannot fail to live up to his profession. Being himself 'the power of God and the wisdom of God,' he has both the knowledge and the will to teach. The disciple who believes that he is who he is can commit himself to Christ's teaching with complete certainty, and without fear of disappointment. He can have complete confidence in Christ's words, even when he does not fully understand them and even when they sound unrealistic.

If he not only listens to Christ's teaching but also obeys it, he will know, from his own experience, that it makes sense. He will recognise that it is indeed a gift of divine wisdom. And he will have no cause to fear the judgment, because he will be like the man who built his house on rock.

Prayer

In you, Lord Jesus, my Master, I have placed my trust, and I know that I shall not be disappointed. Grant me such perfect understanding of your teaching that I may be able to pass it on to others.

18

THE OBSCURITY OF FAITH

The Faith of Abraham

God tested Abraham, and said to him, "Abraham!" And he said, "Here am I." He said, "Take your son, your only son Isaac, whom you love, and go to the land of Moriah, and offer him there as a burnt offering upon one of the mountains of which I shall tell you." So Abraham rose early in the morning, saddled his ass, and took two of his young men with him, and his son Isaac; and he cut the wood for the burnt offering, and arose and went to the place of which God had told him. On the third day Abraham lifted up his eyes and saw the place afar off. Then Abraham said to his young men, "Stay here with the ass; I and the lad will go yonder and worship, and come again to you." And Abraham took the wood of the burnt offering, and laid it on Isaac his son; and he took in his hand the fire and the knife. So they went both of them together. And Isaac said to his father Abraham, "My father!" And he said, "Here am I, my son." He said, "Behold, the fire and the wood; but where is the lamb for a burnt offering?" Abraham said, "God will provide himself the lamb for a burnt offering, my son." So they went both of them together.

When they came to the place of which God had told him, Abraham built an altar there, and laid the wood in order, and bound Isaac his son, and laid him on the altar,

upon the wood. Then Abraham put forth his hand, and took the knife to slay his son. But the angel of the Lord called to him from heaven, and said, "Abraham, Abraham!" And he said, "Here am I." He said, "Do not lay your hand on the lad or do anything to him; for now I know that you fear God, seeing you have not withheld your son, your only son, from me."

(Gen 22:1-12)

The Faith of Mary

The angel said to Mary, "Do not be afraid, Mary, for you have found favour with God. And behold, you will conceive in your womb and bear a son, and you shall call his name Jesus.

He will be great, and will be called the Son of the Most High; and the Lord God will give to him the throne of his father David, and he will reign over the house of Jacob for ever; and of his kingdom there will be no end."

And Mary said to the angel, "How can this be, since I have no husband?" And the angel said to her, "The Holy Spirit will come upon you, and the power of the Most High will overshadow you; therefore the child to be born will be called holy, the Son of God.

And behold, your kinswoman Elizabeth in her old age has also conceived a son; and this is the sixth month with her who was called barren. For with God nothing will be impossible." And Mary said, "Behold, I am the handmaid of the Lord; let it be to me according to your word." And the angel departed from her.

(Lk 1:30-38)

Reflection

At the beginning of the history of Israel, God raised up a great example and prototype of faith: Abraham trusted

God absolutely, and continued to obey, even when what God ordered was incomprehensible to him. At the beginning of his life, God told him to get up and go from Ur of the Chaldees to an unknown destination—'to the land which I will show you' (Gen 12:1). He got up and went. Later, God gave him a son and heir, Isaac, and promised possession of the Holy Land to Isaac and his descendants. The greatest test of all came at the end of Abraham's life, when he was commanded to sacrifice his only son Isaac, through whom the promises were to be fulfilled. The command was astounding: God seemed to be repudiating his oft-repeated promises and going back on his word. Abraham could not understand, but he did not allow himself to doubt God's fidelity to his promises. In the darkness of incomprehension he prepared to fulfil God's commands.

Throughout the centuries, the faith of Israel was put to the test in much the same way: the justice of God was hard to discern in the pattern of history: the worst of the kings, Manasseh, died in his bed; but Josiah, the best of them was killed in battle (cf 2 Kgs 23:26). The Book of Job is entirely concerned with this problem: What has become of the justice of God? Job persisted in his faith in God even when all appearances were against the wisdom of it.

At the beginning of the history of the Church, God gave us another fine example of faith in the Annunciation to Mary, the Mother of Jesus. According to the law of Moses, a woman who was unfaithful during the time of her betrothal was liable to death by stoning. Mary, though perfectly innocent, was liable to fall under this suspicion; and as far as she could see, the destiny to which she was called would mean the end of her marriage to Joseph. Her *Fiat* was a word of great courage, by which she committed her life to God's care in the midst of danger and uncertitudes.

Mary is a model of what every Christian should strive and pray to become. We must learn from her example to commit our lives into God's hand, saying: 'Behold the servant (or handmaid) of the Lord!' And we must do so with joy, as she did: 'My soul magnifies the Lord, and my spirit rejoices in God my saviour'. Joy too is a gift of the Spirit, springing from strong, courageous faith. At the present time, perhaps, we cannot understand what God is doing, either in our own life or in the Church. He may seem to have deserted us. But the example of patriarchs and saints reassures us: the God of Israel does not sleep. Even when most invisible, he is very close at hand.

Prayer

Give us the humility to believe, O Lord, that even though it is not clear to us, the universe is unfolding as it should, and all is safely in your keeping.

19

A HIDDEN EPIPHANY

A Misty Mirror

Our knowledge is imperfect and our prophecy is imperfect; but when the perfect comes, the imperfect will pass away. When I was a child, I spoke like a child, I thought like a child, I reasoned like a child; when I became a man, I gave up childish ways. For now we see in a mirror dimly, but then face to face. Now I know in part; then I shall understand fully, even as I have been fully understood.

(1 Cor 13:9-12)

A Disappointing Revelation?

"Let not your hearts be troubled; believe in God, believe also in me. In my Father's house are many rooms; if it were not so, would I have told you that I go to prepare a place for you? And when I go and prepare a place for you, I will come again and will take you to myself, that where I am you may be also. And you know the way where I am going." Thomas said to him, "Lord, we do not know where you are going; how can we know the way?" Jesus said to him, "I am the way, and the truth, and the life; no one comes to the Father, but by me. If you had known me, you would have known my Father also; henceforth you know him and have seen him."

Philip said to him, "Lord, show us the Father, and we shall be satisfied." Jesus said to him, "Have I been with

you so long, and yet you do not know me, Philip? He who has seen me has seen the Father; how can you say, 'Show us the Father'? Do you not believe that I am in the Father and the Father in me? The words that I say to you I do not speak on my own authority; but the Father who dwells in me does his works. Believe me that I am in the Father and the Father in me; or else believe me for the sake of the works themselves.

(Jn 14:1-11)

Reflection

Our faith is obscure in various ways. There is the obscurity of incomprehension, when we cannot understand what God is doing (cf Ps 14)—of which the extreme case is the testing of Abraham. But our faith is also obscure because the revelation to which it responds is obscure—so much so that Philip did not recognise it as revelation. God did not give the revelation which men wanted; he gave us what we needed. What we would like—what Philip and Jude asked for at the Last Supper—is a revelation of the glory, majesty and beauty of God, like the Transfiguration. The disciples were probably disappointed with Christ's answer to Philip: 'You have seen him already; he who has seen me has seen the Father.' The glorious epiphany they wanted is reserved to the end of time. God in his providence chose to reveal something other than his glory: he sent his Son to empty himself of his glory and set an example of obedience. He wanted to give us, not something to wonder at, but someone to imitate. He wanted to set before us a model of God-like conduct—to show us what a man is like if his conduct is God-like. God the Father is said to have revealed himself in Christ, because Christ always acted in a God-like way, for our instruction. This kind of revelation gives us practical knowledge of God—knowledge we can act upon. By comparison with the glorious revelation which we should like, it was an obscure and even a disappointing revelation. But the man of faith

overcomes this disappointment; he believes that God is good and God knows best.

Again, our faith is obscure because Christ uttered 'mysteries' which he did not explain. He told Nicodemus, for example, that a man is reborn and transformed in baptism, but he did not explain how this is done nor what our new life is like. So even our own being as Christians is a mystery hidden with Christ in God.

The reward and consummation, or transfiguration, of our faith will be the final revelation of these revealed yet concealed mysteries. We live between two revelations. Christ's past, obscure revelation implants in us a faith which looks forward confidently to the final, glorious epiphany. As a result of the first revelation we see through a glass obscurely; then we shall see face to face.

Prayer

Lead us, O Lord, by the kindly light of your Spirit, through the obscurities of this life, to the revelation of your glory; renew our strength and courage, lest we faint by the way.

20

DIFFICULTIES AND DOUBTS

The Problem of Israel's Unbelief

I am speaking the truth in Christ, I am not lying; my conscience bears me witness in the Holy Spirit, that I have great sorrow and unceasing anguish in my heart. For I could wish that I myself were accursed and cut off from Christ for the sake of my brethren, my kinsmen by race. They are Israelites, and to them belong the sonship, the glory, the covenants, the giving of the law, the worship, and the promises; to them belong the patriarchs, and of their race, according to the flesh, is the Christ, who is God over all, blessed for ever. Amen.

But it is not as though the word of God had failed. For not all who are descended from Israel belong to Israel.
(Rom 9:1-6)

Saviour or Sinner?

Now it was a sabbath day when Jesus made the clay and opened the man's eyes. The Pharisees again asked him how he had received his sight. And he said to them, "He put clay on my eyes, and I washed, and I see." Some of the Pharisees said, "This man is not from God, for he does not keep the sabbath." But others said, "How can a man who is a sinner do such signs?" There was a division among them. So they again said to the blind man, "What do

you say about him, since he has opened your eyes?" He said, "He is a prophet."

The Jews did not believe that he had been blind and had received his sight, until they called the parents of the man who had received his sight, and asked them, "Is this your son, who you say was born blind? How then does he now see?" His parents answered, "We know that this is our son, and that he was born blind; but how he now sees we do not know, nor do we know who opened his eyes. Ask him; he is of age, he will speak for himself." His parents said this because they feared the Jews, for the Jews had already agreed that if any one should confess him to be Christ, he was to be put out of the synagogue. Therefore his parents said, "He is of age, ask him."

So for the second time they called the man who had been blind, and said to him, "Give God the praise; we know that this man is a sinner." He answered, "Whether he is a sinner, I do not know; one thing I know, that though I was blind, now I see." They said to him, "What did he do to you? How did he open your eyes?" He answered them, "I have told you already, and you would not listen. Why do you want to hear it again? Do you too want to become his disciples?" And they reviled him, saying, "You are his disciple, but we are disciples of Moses. We know that God has spoken to Moses, but as for this man, we do not know where he comes from." The man answered, "Why, this is a marvel! You do not know where he comes from, and yet he opened my eyes. We know that God does not listen to sinners, but if any one is a worshipper of God and does his will, God listens to him. Never since the world began has it been heard that any one opened the eyes of a man born blind. If this man were not from God, he could do nothing." They answered him, "You were born in utter sin, and would you teach us?" And they cast him out.

(Jn 9:14-34)

Reflection

The believer is never free from difficulties, but difficulties are not the same as doubts. There is a much-quoted saying of Cardinal Newman that 'ten thousand difficulties do not make a doubt.' Some people say this is not true; but it *is* true—and very important.

What is meant is illustrated by the readings from St Paul and St John. To take first the gospel passage: the cured man believes in Jesus as a prophet because he knows that he has been cured by Jesus; he reasons that only a prophet could do such a thing. The Pharisees try to undermine his faith by proposing difficulties: Jesus is a law-breaker, therefore he cannot be a prophet; and if they, the expert theologians, do not believe that Jesus is a prophet, will the blind man set his opinion against their authority? The cured man does not attempt to resolve these difficulties; they remain difficulties. But he holds on firmly, without doubting, to the positive grounds of his faith: 'Whether he is a sinner, I wouldn't know. One thing I do know—that I was a blind man and now I see." He sees the difficulties, but they do not make him doubt. If he had said: 'Bless my soul! You Pharisees may be right! I had better reconsider the matter'—that would have been doubt. Doubt is the suspension of assent. But the blind man decides to hold on resolutely to his faith, looking to its positive grounds and discounting the objections.

St Paul, too, was confronted with difficulties. He firmly believed that Jesus was the Messiah, the promised Son of Abraham, in whom and through whom all the great promises of the Old Testament were being fulfilled. And yet the Jews as a whole were rejecting the gospel! What was God doing? Had he abandoned his people? Had he renounced his covenants? This problem tortured St Paul—he discusses it all through chapter 9-11 of Romans. He could not find a fully satisfying solution. But he never wavered in his faith, because he held on firmly to the positive grounds of his

belief, namely, his memory of the Damascus vision and his experience of the Holy Spirit in the Church.

Our assent is a free act. If we are foolish enough to give the whole of our attention to the difficulties we encounter, we shall be tempted to renounce our faith. It is important therefore, that we should remind ourselves more often of the good reasons we have for persevering in our faith. 'One thing I know—I was a blind man and now I see.'

Prayer

Give us the strength and wisdom, O Lord, to believe without doubting whatever you have revealed; and help us to resolve, through prayer and patient reflection, the difficulties which beset our faith.

21

UNDERSTANDING TOO IS A GIFT

Love seeks Understanding

If I speak in the tongues of men and of angels, but have not love, I am a noisy gong or a clanging cymbal. And if I have prophetic powers, and understand all mysteries and all knowledge, and if I have all faith, so as to remove mountains, but have not love, I am nothing. If I give away all I have, and if I deliver my body to be burned, but have not love, I gain nothing.

Love is patient and kind; love is not jealous, or boastful; it is not arrogant or rude. Love does not insist on its own way; it is not irritable or resentful; it does not rejoice at wrong, but rejoices in the right. Love bears all things, believes all things, hopes all things, endures all things.

Love never ends; as for prophecies, they will pass away; as for tongues, they will cease; as for knowledge, it will pass away. For our knowledge is imperfect and our prophecy is imperfect; but when the perfect comes, the imperfect will pass away. When I was a child, I spoke like a child, I thought like a child, I reasoned like a child; when I became a man, I gave up childish ways. For now we see in a mirror dimly, but then face to face. Now I know in part; then I shall understand fully, even as I have been fully understood. So faith, hope, love abide, these three; but the greatest of these is love.

(1 Cor 13:1-13)

The Blind Man sees Best

Taking the twelve, Jesus said to them, "Behold, we are going up to Jerusalem, and everything that is written of the Son of man by the prophets will be accomplished. For he will be delivered to the Gentiles, and will be mocked and shamefully treated and spat upon; they will scourge him and kill him, and on the third day he will rise." But they understood none of these things; this saying was hid from them, and they did not grasp what was said.

As he drew near Jericho, a blind man was sitting by the roadside begging; and hearing a multitude going by, he inquired what this meant. They told him, "Jesus of Nazareth is passing by." And he cried, "Jesus, Son of David, have mercy on me!" And those who were in front rebuked him, telling him to be silent; but he cried out all the more; "Son of David, have mercy on me!" And Jesus stopped, and commanded him to be brought to him; and when he came near, he asked him, "What do you want me to do for you?" He said, "Lord, let me receive my sight." And Jesus said to him, "Receive your sight; your faith has made you well." And immediately he received his sight and followed him, glorifying God; and all the people, when they saw it, gave praise to God.

(Lk 18:31-43)

Reflection

This passage of the gospel presents a most remarkable contrast: Jesus speaks plainly to his disciples about the details of his passion, and about his resurrection; and the words make no impression on them—they simply do not understand. He gives them in advance the lesson he will later give to the two on the road to Emmaus, and their eyes fail them: they cannot see what he means. Then, as he enters Jericho, a blind man realizes who he is and cries

out: 'Son of David, have mercy on me!' The blind man recognises Jesus as Messiah and Saviour, while the disciples remain blind. There is something preternatural about his seeing and their blindness.

It is exactly the same when Jesus' prophecy is fulfilled: when the chief priests have handed him over to Pilate, and he has been mocked, spat upon and scourged, and brought out wearing the red cloak, Pilate says: 'Behold your king,' but the Jews cannot see it; in their blindness they cry out for Barabbas. And at that very time, according to St Matthew, Pilate's wife sends a message that she has learned in a dream, during the night, with her eyes shut, that Jesus is an innocent man. A sleeping gentile woman sees better than Israel!

These incidents show that not only is faith a gift of God, but understanding is a gift too. People see without seeing, and they hear without hearing. What of ourselves? We like to think that we have faith, and we understand the gospel well enough; we have learned what there is to learn. But can we be sure? St Paul says that we see in a glass darkly. But is it not likely that some men see in the glass of faith more clearly than others? What can we do in order to see more clearly? Perhaps three things: first, we can make our own the prayer of the blind man: 'Jesus, son of David, have mercy on me! Lord, that I may see!' Secondly, since St Paul says that faith without love is useless, we can try to look upon Christ with greater love. It is impossible to get knowledge of a *person* without love. And thirdly, Jesus says in the Sermon on the Mount: 'Blessed are the pure in heart, for they shall *see God*.' Perhaps that promise has its fulfilment in this life as well as in the next. Today, let us try to be pure in heart—to be chaste in thought, and to have a pure intention of seeking the glory of God by prayers, fasting and almsdeeds that are known to God alone.

Prayer

O Lord, the Creator of Light, remove the veil from our mind's eyes, so that we may see the truth and beauty of the revelation which you have set before us.

22

FAITH IS A VICTORY

The World is Hostile

Every one who believes that Jesus is the Christ is a child of God, and every one who loves the parent loves the child. By this we know that we love the children of God, when we love God and obey his commandments. For this is the love of God, that we keep his commandments. And his commandments are not burdensome. For whatever is born of God overcomes the world; and this is the victory that overcomes the world, our faith. Who is it that overcomes the world but he who believes that Jesus is the Son of God?

(1 Jn 5:1-5)

Faith put to a Test

Martha said to Jesus, "Lord, if you had been here, my brother would not have died. And even now I know that whatever you ask from God, God will give you." Jesus said to her, "Your brother will rise again." Martha said to him, "I know that he will rise again in the resurrection at the last day." Jesus said to her, "I am the resurrection and the life; he who believes in me, though he die, yet shall he live, and whoever lives and believes in me shall never die. Do you believe this?" She said to him, "Yes, Lord; I believe that you are the Christ, the Son of God, he who is coming into the world." *(Jn 11:21-27)*

Reflection

Because of its obscurity, faith is not easy. The life of faith involves self-conquest, as can be seen in the lives of Abraham and of Job. To a lesser degree the same is true of all believers. We are put to the test of time, and perhaps to the test of disappointment and of suffering.

It may surprise us that God should want to test us in this way, since we do not deliberately test the fidelity of those whom we love. But this surprise is itself a test which we must overcome. We have to learn to believe patiently and humbly that God has his own good reasons, which we do not fully understand, when he disappoints us. God the Father wants to test our faith—as we can see from the gospel, for in this too Jesus is the revelation of his Father. He who has seen Jesus in the gospels—for example, in the story of the raising of Lazarus—has seen in him the Father's will to test his disciples. When asked to cure Lazarus, he disappoints Martha and Mary by allowing their brother to die; but Martha's faith remains firm. She says: '*Even now* I believe that whatever you ask, God will do for you,' and in spite of her disappointment she still confesses Jesus as Messiah and Son of God. Then at last her faith is rewarded. Jesus even tests his own mother in this way. At Cana, he first seems to refuse her request—almost rudely: 'Woman, what is it to me and to thee?' But she does not lose heart, and her trust is rewarded.

These and other incidents in the gospel (for example, the story of the Syrophoenician woman) show that it is better, in the end, for the believer to have been put to the test. No virtue is of much value until it has been tested. The man who has been through a trial and has survived it is a better man than one who has not been tempted. Virtues are not acquired by verbal profession of them but by the practice of them in testing conditions. That is why the author of the Epistle to the Hebrews can say that Christ learned obedience through suffering. There is no

other way. One does not learn obedience by saying: 'O God, I would rather die a thousand deaths than disobey you,' but only by obeying, and particularly by obeying when one's natural inclination is to rebel. The cross of Christ is our supreme example: God the Father, out of love for his Son, allowed him to be put to the supreme test, so that he could give a supreme proof of his fidelity, obedience and love. That is how he was made perfect.

In the passage from the First Epistle of St John, faith is described, rather mysteriously, as a victory over the world: 'This is the victory that overcomes the world: our faith.' The meaning is, no doubt, that our faith is a continual victory over the world, because the world constantly entices us, and we overcome it by renouncing and refusing its enticements. We are constantly faced with the choice of two masters, and must constantly and resolutely reaffirm our decision to renounce the world (or Satan) and obey Christ. In this sense, faith requires a constant renewal of decision.

Prayer

Lead us not into temptation, O Lord; but if it is your will that our faith be tested by disappointment, give us the strength to pass the test, to your greater glory.

23

SELF-DEFLATING WISDOM

Sophisticated Terminologies Superfluous

The word of the cross is folly to those who are perishing, but to us who are being saved it is the power of God. For it is written, "I will destroy the wisdom of the wise, and the cleverness of the clever I will thwart." Where is the wise man? Where is the scribe? Where is the debater of this age? Has not God made foolish the wisdom of the world? For since, in the wisdom of God, the world did not know God through wisdom, it pleased God through the folly of what we preach to save those who believe. For Jews demand signs and Greeks seek wisdom, but we preach Christ crucified, a stumbling block to Jews and folly to Gentiles, but to those who are called, both Jews and Greeks, Christ the power of God and the wisdom of God. For the foolishness of God is wiser than men, and the weakness of God is stronger than men.

(1 Cor 1:18-25)

A More Mysterious Religion

Now there was a man of the Pharisees, named Nicodemus, a ruler of the Jews. This man came to Jesus by night and said to him, "Rabbi, we know that you are a teacher come from God; for no one can do these signs that you do, unless God is with him." Jesus answered him, "Truly, truly, I say to you unless one is born anew, he cannot see the kingdom

of God." Nicodemus said to him, "How can a man be born when he is old? Can he enter a second time into his mother's womb and be born?" Jesus answered, "Truly, truly, I say to you, unless one is born of water and the Spirit, he cannot enter the kingdom of God. That which is born of the flesh is flesh, and that which is born of the the Spirit is spirit. Do not marvel that I said to you, 'You must be born anew.' The wind blows where it wills, and you hear the sound of it, but you do not know whence it comes or whither it goes; so it is with every one who is born of the Spirit." Nicodemus said to him, "How can this be?" Jesus answered him, "Are you a teacher of Israel, and yet you do not understand this? Truly, truly, I say to you, we speak of what we know, and bear witness to what we have seen; but you do not receive our testimony. If I have told you earthly things and you do not believe, how can you believe if I tell you heavenly things? No one has ascended into heaven but he who descended from heaven, the Son of man. And as Moses lifted up the serpent in the wilderness, so must the Son of man be lifted up, that whoever believes in him may have eternal life. For God so loved the world that he gave his only Son, that whoever believes in him should not perish but have eternal life."

(Jn 3:1-16)

Reflection

Our reason would like to be autonomous: we should like to be able to think everything out for ourselves, and not have to accept important truths on hearsay, especially after a long period of tradition. Whoever accepts the gospel is required not only to trust the word of others but also to accept doctrines which sound improbable and incomprehensible—such as our rebirth in baptism, or the future resurrection of our bodies.

Christ's words to Nicodemus show that he did not intend his disciples to understand all that they have to believe. He

intended them to accept some things ('earthly things' like the efficacy of baptism, and 'heavenly things' like the efficacy of his death) simply on faith, as a proof of their willingness to trust him. Christianity is a much more mysterious religion than Judaism, because the disciple of Christ is required to accept many more 'hard words' on sheer faith.

However, we must not draw a sharp contrast between Judaism as a straightforward, intelligible religion which commends itself to reason, and Christianity as a complicated and mysterious religion which affronts and humiliates reason. The evangelists take pains to show that the introduction of mysteries into the relationship between God and man was not a radical break with the Jewish tradition. St John in his prologue reminds his reader that the Old Testament knew of a mysterious figure called Sophia (Wisdom) or Logos (Word), who was at work in the creation of the world (cf Prov 8:22-31). St Peter in his first Epistle (3:20-21) points out that water was the instrument of salvation for Noah; and St Paul implies the same when he speaks of the crossing of the Red Sea as a type prophecy of baptism (cf 1 Cor 10:2). In the discourse to Nicodemus, Jesus points to the sacrifice of Isaac and to the raising-up of the Brazen Serpent as types of the sacrifice of the Cross. So it cannot be said that Jesus transformed Judaism into a mystery religion; it had its own mysteries already. But the mysterious element is much larger in the teaching of Jesus than in any of the Hebrew prophets.

St Paul tries to explain this feature of the gospel in the passage from First Corinthians. He argues that God did not wish to minister to human pride by giving a gospel which only the wise and the learned could understand. If he had done that, he would have given them something fresh to boast about. But God hates man's pride and boasting. He hates the wisdom that puffs men up with pride and exalts them above their fellows. He has punished the proud by making their salvation dependant on accept-

ance of a gospel which they have rendered themselves incapable of accepting. At the same time he has given to the simple a saving message which, by reason of its content, should preserve them from getting puffed up with pride. The better they understand it, the less inclined will they be to pride themselves on their knowledge.

In his First Epistle to the Corinthians, St Paul sees that the Christians of Corinth *are* beginning to get puffed up with their superior wisdom. He points out the folly of it: Christ himself was crucified; the apostles are regarded as the scum of the earth; yet the Corinthians pride themselves on their knowledge (*gnôsis*) of the gospel! If they really understood it, they could not be proud. Christians have wisdom of their own (cf 1 Cor 2:6), but it was never meant to puff them up. By reason of its content, it should be a self-deflating wisdom.

Prayer

Give us, O Lord, the simplicity of children, so that we may accept the mysteries of your kingdom with wonder and gratitude; may we bless when we understand, and still bless you when we do not; may we bless you when you give, and still bless when you take away.

24

REVELATION OF JUSTICE AND SINFULNESS

The Vindication of Jesus

I hope to come to you soon, but I am writing these instructions to you so that, if I am delayed, you may know how one ought to behave in the household of God, which is the church of the living God, the pillar and bulwark of the truth. Great indeed, we confess, is the mystery of our religion: He was manifested in the flesh, vindicated in the Spirit, seen by angels, preached among the nations, believed on in the world, taken up in glory.

(1 Tim 3:14-16)

The Work of the Paraclete

"I did not say these things to you from the beginning, because I was with you. But now I am going to him who sent me; yet none of you asks me, 'Where are you going?' But because I have said these things to you, sorrow has filled your hearts. Nevertheless I tell you the truth: it is to your advantage that I go away, for if I do not go away, the Counsellor will not come to you; but if I go, I will send him to you. And when he comes, he will convince the world of sin and of righteousness and of judgment: of sin, because they do not believe in me; of righteousness, because I go to the Father, and you will see me no more; of judgment, because the ruler of this world is judged.

"I have yet many things to say to you, but you cannot bear them now. When the Spirit of truth comes, he will guide you into all the truth; for he will not speak on his own authority, but whatever he hears he will speak, and he will declare to you the things that are to come. He will glorify me, for he will take what is mine and declare it to you."

(Jn 16:4-14)

Reflection

During his own ministry, Jesus tried to convince the Jewish world of sin and of justice: of the sinfulness of man, and of the justice of God—that God is not indifferent to what goes on in this world, that he watches and records, and that he will one day judge the world (that is, all men) in righteousness. And man is not ready to face God's judgment: he mistakes God's patience for indifference; he tells himself that all is well, when he ought to be beating his breast and asking for mercy.

Jesus tried to bring these things home to the Jews during his ministry, but for the most part they did not believe. One of the reasons why it was expedient that he should go to the Father was that he was to teach these things much more effectively through his Holy Spirit and through the teaching of his apostles. He had a much greater effect on his own people after his death and resurrection than he did during his ministry.

His death and resurrection were the greatest demonstration of the sinfulness of man and of the justice of God. God sent his own Son into the world to be our teacher, and how did sinful men react? They made themselves superlatively sinful by rejecting him and crucifying him. But God showed his righteousness by raising his obedient Son from the dead and glorifying him at his right hand. The resurrection was his vindication. It was by pointing back to the cross and resurrection that the apostles con-

vinced the world of sin and of justice—as can be seen, for example, from St Peter's discourse at Pentecost: he tells the Jews that 'Jesus whom you crucified' is at God's right hand pouring out the gift of the Holy Spirit. They are stung with remorse; two thousand ask for baptism.

This is still the message of the Holy Spirit—that man is under the judgment of God, that we are a sinful race, in need of forgiveness and redemption. Let us invite and implore the Holy Spirit to imprint these truths in our hearts, so that we may be duly humble before God. As soon as we accept God's judgment and humble ourselves, he comes to meet us and gives us the spirit of forgiveness —and that means a spirit of joy and peace. The peace of Christ is attained through sorrow for sin. 'Blessed are those who mourn, for they shall be comforted.'

Prayer

Wash us yet more, O Lord, from our sins, so that we need not fear the day of judgment; let it not be for us a day of darkness and remorse, but a day of joyful revelation, as we enter into your peace.

25

FAITH AND MORALITY

The Pauline Privilege

To the rest I say, not the Lord, that if any brother has a wife who is an unbeliever, and she consents to live with him, he should not divorce her. If any woman has a husband who is an unbeliever, and he consents to live with her, she should not divorce him. For the unbelieving husband is consecrated through his wife, and the unbelieving wife is consecrated through her husband. Otherwise, your children would be unclean, but as it is they are holy. But if the unbelieving partner desires to separate, let it be so; in such a case the brother or sister is not bound. For God has called us to peace. Wife, how do you know whether you will save your husband? Husband, how do you know whether you will save your wife?

Only, let every one lead the life which the Lord has assigned to him, and in which God has called him. This is my rule in all the churches.

(1 Cor 7:12-17)

Prohibition of Divorce

Pharisees came up to him and tested him by asking, "Is it lawful to divorce one's wife for any cause?" He answered, "Have you not read that he who made them from the beginning made them male and female, and said, 'For this reason a man shall leave his father and mother and be

joined to his wife, and the two shall become one'? So they are no longer two but one. What therefore God has joined together, let no man put asunder." They said to him, "Why then did Moses command one to give a certificate of divorce, and to put her away?" He said to them, "For your hardness of heart Moses allowed you to divorce your wives, but from the beginning it was not so. And I say to you: whoever divorces his wife, except for unchastity, and marries another, commits adultery; and he who marries a divorced woman commits adultery."

The disciples said to him, "If such is the case of a man with his wife, it is not expedient to marry." But he said to them, "Not all men can receive this precept, but only those to whom it is given."

(Mt 19:3-11)

Reflection

We often talk about 'faith and morals' as if these two things were quite distinct from each other—as if Christian morality were not a matter of faith—as if in the field of morality we were free to follow our own judgment. But the gospels show that when Jesus spoke about questions of morality, he spoke as a revealer, and expected his teaching to be accepted on faith, because of his authority.

When speaking on divorce, he does not argue from reason, like a moral philosopher. He compares one text of the Pentateuch with another—chapter 24 of Deuteronomy with chapter 2 of Genesis—and reveals that the original will of God was that marriage should be indissoluble; there was to be no divorce with freedom to remarry. When the disciples exclaim that marriage on such terms would be intolerable, Jesus does not reason with them, but takes up their words in a paradoxical sense and gives another piece of teaching which is to be accepted on faith.

In the Sermon on the Mount, Jesus is revealing the conditions of entry into the kingdom of heaven. These

cannot be discovered by natural moral reason. Jesus reveals them; and in so doing he also reveals that the moral standards of most men are too low: 'The gate that leads to destruction is wide, the road is broad, and many go that way.' Jesus does not tell the many that they may freely follow their permissive consciences—far from it! He warns them that they are on the road to ruin, and reveals the very high standards which will be required at the judgment in those who are to be admitted to the kingdom. In a word, their conduct must be God-like: they must show themselves to be true sons of their Father in heaven. Because Jesus knows the Father, he can describe what God-like conduct means, and he can pass judgment on the conduct and teaching of the Pharisees.

In view of Christ's universal prohibition of divorce, it is hard to see how St Paul could feel justified in granting the Pauline privilege. Theologians are still hard put to it to explain how he could do this. But the Church has always accepted his ruling because of his apostolic authority —which again shows that Christian morality is based on faith. We do not think out for ourselves the rules we live by; we listen to Christ and his apostles telling us the rules we must obey, if we want to enter the kingdom of heaven.

Prayer

Preserve us in the spirit of faith, Lord Jesus; and grant that we may learn by experience that your way is the way of wisdom, that your commandments are not grievous, and that you are indeed the Light of the world.

26

FAITH WORKING THROUGH CHARITY

Preparation for Service

When Christ appeared as a high priest of the good things that have come, then through the greater and more perfect tent (not made with hands, that is, not of this creation) he entered once for all into the Holy Place, taking not the blood of goats and calves but his own blood, thus securing an eternal redemption. For if the sprinkling of defiled persons with the blood of goats and bulls and with the ashes of a heifer sanctifies for the purification of the flesh, how much more shall the blood of Christ, who through the eternal Spirit offered himself without blemish to God, purify your conscience from dead works to serve the living God.

(Heb 9:11-14)

The Saviour warns the Saved

There was a feast of the Jews, and Jesus went up to Jerusalem.

Now there is in Jerusalem by the Sheep Gate a pool, in Hebrew called Bethzatha, which has five porticoes. In these lay a multitude of invalids, blind, lame, paralyzed. One man was there, who had been ill for thirty-eight years. When Jesus saw him and knew that he had been lying there a long time, he said to him, "Do you want to be healed?" The sick man answered him, "Sir, I have no

man to put me into the pool when the water is troubled, and while I am going another steps down before me." Jesus said to him, "Rise, take up your pallet, and walk." And at once the man was healed, and he took up his pallet and walked.

Now that day was the sabbath. So the Jews said to the man who was cured, "It is the sabbath, it is not lawful for you to carry your pallet." But he answered them, "The man who healed me said to me, 'Take up your pallet, and walk.'" They asked him, "Who is the man who said to you, 'Take up your pallet, and walk'?" Now the man who had been healed did not know who it was, for Jesus had withdrawn, as there was a crowd in the place. Afterward, Jesus found him in the temple, and said to him, "See, you are well! Sin no more, that nothing worse befall you."
(Jn 5:1-14)

Reflection

St Paul's proclamation of freedom from law has always been open to misunderstanding. He has been taken to mean that for those who believe, violations of the ten commandments are no longer sins, since they have passed out of the realm of law into a new world of grace where there is no law. In more than one of his Epistles he attempts to show that he is not guilty of teaching this libertine or antinomian version of Christianity. As he says in the Epistle to the Galatians (5:6), faith must express itself in charity. But charity requires obedience to the decalogue (cf Rom 13:8).

The reading from the Epistle to the Hebrews makes the same point: the death of Christ cleanses us from our past deeds of death. It should be a once-and-for-all cleansing, after which we serve the living God by obedience to his commands. What we are offered is not a weekly baptism, so that we can continue forever in unregenerate ways.

Perhaps the point is made even more clearly in the passage from St John: the man is raised up from a state of sickness and weakness bordering on death; he is given life and strength—but not to use or misuse as he pleases. He is to sin no more, lest something worse than thirty-eight years of sickness be imposed upon him as punishment. The life given to us through the sacraments is in the same way given to us for a purpose: we are to walk steadily in the ways of God's commandments. If we misuse the life that is given to us, and vex the Holy Spirit within us, the last state is likely to be worse than the first. Christians must not sigh for the flesh-pots of Egypt, on which they have turned their backs; they must press on to the promised land. They must show themselves worthy of admission to the kingdom by imitating the gentleness, chastity and obedience of Christ.

Prayer

May your love for us, revealed in your death, inspire us, Lord Jesus, to spend ourselves in the love and service of our fellow men. You saved us at great cost to yourself; may we too serve our neighbour at some cost to ourselves.

27

A KINGDOM OF PRIESTS

The Word of the Lord is for All

It shall come to pass in the latter days that the mountain of the house of the Lord shall be established as the highest of the mountains, and shall be raised above the hills; and all the nations shall flow to it, and many peoples shall come, and say: "Come, let us go up to the mountain of the Lord, to the house of the God of Jacob; that he may teach us his ways and that we may walk in his paths." For out of Zion shall go forth the law, and the word of the Lord from Jerusalem. He shall judge between the nations, and shall decide for many peoples; and they shall beat their swords into ploughshares, and their spears into pruning hooks; nation shall not lift up sword against nation, neither shall they learn war any more.

(Isa 2:2-4)

A City on a Hill

"You are the salt of the earth; but if salt has lost its taste, how shall its saltness be restored? It is no longer good for anything except to be thrown out and trodden under foot by men.

"You are the light of the world. A city set on a hill cannot be hid. Nor do men light a lamp and put it under a bushel, but on a stand, and it gives light to all in the house.

Let your light so shine before men, that they may see your good works and give glory to your Father who is in heaven."

(Mt 5:13-16)

Reflection

When God chose the Israelites to be his own people, he chose them for a priestly, mediatorial mission. They were to be 'a kingdom of priests and a holy people' (Exod 19:6) —holy in that they were to seek to be holy as God is holy, and perfect as God is perfect. Their priestly function is to mediate knowledge of God's will to their descendants and to other nations.

Under the monarchy, the Jews failed to fulfil this priestly ministry. Far from causing the name of Yahweh to be glorified among the nations, they brought him into disgrace. The sins of Israel were punished by a series of national calamities culminating in the fall of Jerusalem to Nebuchadnezzar in 587 B.C. This gave the Gentiles no very favourable impression of Yahweh's power to save his people.

But Isaiah knew that after the punishment would come restoration. One day the Jews would be reestablished in Jerusalem and would fulfil their mission. Through their obedience to the law, Mount Sion (on which Jerusalem is built) would shine out as the resting place of the glory of God, and Gentiles would come from afar to learn God's will from Israel.

In the Sermon on the Mount, Jesus tells his disciples that the destiny of Israel is to be fulfilled in them—*they* are to constitute the city built on a hill which will command the attention of all men. When men see their unity and charity, they will give glory to God and seek instruction in the Christian way of life. A community of Christians should always display a higher standard of justice and charity than is accepted by the unbelieving mass of mankind.

This comparative element is essential to Christian morality. Belief in the world to come, and in God working within them, should make Christians a leaven, which will gradually transform the whole mass of mankind.

The Christian religion should foster an improvement in the morality of all men. As St Paul says, we should shine out as a beacon amidst a crooked and adulterous generation (cf Phil 2:15). In some ways, we can see this happening; thanks in part at least to the efforts of Christians, the general public is much more concerned about the poor and underprivileged now than at the beginning of the century. But we have no cause to be pleased with ourselves. Our faith should work itself out in charity (cf Gal 5:6) more strikingly than it does. We must seek the glory of God alone; but men must see our good works and give glory (not to us) but to our Father in heaven.

Prayer

Through obedience to your teaching, Lord Jesus, and through attentive listening to the promptings of your Spirit, may we mediate to other men the knowledge of your revelation.

28

FAITH IN THE PRIESTHOOD

The Promise of Forgiveness

"Behold, the days are coming, says the Lord, when I will make a new covenant with the house of Israel and the house of Judah, not like the covenant which I made with their fathers when I took them by the hand to bring them out of the land of Egypt, my covenant which they broke, though I was their husband, says the Lord. But this is the covenant which I will make with the house of Israel after those days, says the Lord: I will put my law within them, and I will write it upon their hearts; and I will be their God, and they shall be my people. And no longer shall each man teach his neighbour and each his brother, saying, 'Know the Lord,' for they shall all know me, from the least of them to the greatest, says the Lord; for I will forgive their iniquity, and I will remember their sin no more."

(Jer 31:31-34)

The Power to Forgive

On the evening of that day, the first day of the week, the doors being shut where the disciples were, for fear of the Jews, Jesus came and stood among them and said to them, "Peace be with you." When he had said this, he showed them his hands and his side. Then the disciples were glad when they saw the Lord. Jesus said to them again, "Peace

be with you. As the Father has sent me, even so I send you." And when he had said this, he breathed on them, and said to them, "Receive the Holy Spirit. If you forgive the sins of any, they are forgiven; if you retain the sins of any, they are retained."

(Jn 20:19-23)

Reflection

In these ecumenical days we become impatient when anyone starts discussing the validity of these orders or of those. We want to brush aside such 'legalistic' discussions and take a larger, broader view.

But what of the man whose conscience is burdened by sin, and who has suddenly recognised that he is of little value in God's eyes, unless he will seek absolution? Such a man *is* interested in the validity of orders. He knows he cannot absolve himself; he can be forgiven only by God against whom he has sinned, and absolved only by one whom God has authorized to absolve in his name.

The power to absolve was Christ's first gift to his disciples after his resurrection. He then fulfilled the promise of the new covenant uttered by Jeremiah about 600 years before. It is an astounding and precious gift which the successors of those first disciples have inherited: it gives us assurance that our sins are forgiven and restores a peace which we could not otherwise regain. When G. K. Chesterton was asked what brought him into the Roman Catholic Church, he replied: 'The desire of absolution.' The man who deeply desires absolution wants to be very sure that his confessor has power to absolve. It is only because we believe that God is with him that we are willing to kneel at a man's feet and confess our sins.

It was most appropriate for Jesus to give the power to his disciples just after they had failed him in the hour of temptation. Having experienced in their own persons infi-

delity, remorse, repentance and forgiveness, they would know how to be gentle in absolving others. If we can look back in our own lives to occasions when absolution has been the removal of a painful burden of guilt, we shall understand what a great gift the Lord puts into the hands of his priests. In the eyes of many unbelievers the priesthood is a profession hardly worthy of respect; but to those who believe, to the priests and laity, the priestly powers are a wonderful gift from God.

Prayer

We give thanks to you, O Lord our Saviour, who have given such power to the priests of your new covenant that they can cleanse our consciences from deeds of death and fit us to serve you, the living God, in peace and justice.

29

FAITH IN THE CHURCH

Interdependence

As in one body we have many members, and all the members do not have the same function, so we, though many, are one body in Christ, and individually members one of another. Having gifts that differ according to the grace given to us, let us use them: if prophecy, in proportion to our faith; if service, in our serving; he who teaches, in his teaching; he who exhorts, in his exhortation; he who contributes, in liberality; he who gives aid, with zeal; he who does acts of mercy, with cheerfulness.

(Rom 12:4-8)

The Household of Believers

The mother and brethren of Jesus came; and standing outside they sent to him and called him. And a crowd was sitting about him; and they said to him, "Your mother and your brethren are outside, asking for you." And he replied, "Who are my mother and my brethren?" And looking around on those who sat about him, he said, "Here are my mother and my brethren! Whoever does the will of God is my brother and sister, and mother."

(Mk 3:31-35)

Reflection

God has made us human beings interdependent on every level of our being. We depend on our fellow men for food, clothing, fuel, transportation and education. If we were not taught to speak by our parents and family, our thought-processes would be so rudimentary that we should hardly be human. They talk us into humanity.

It should not, therefore, be a surprise to us that in our spiritual life we are equally dependent on one another. Only because we have heard of God's revelation through the words of other men are we able to believe and be justified. No man can baptize himself or absolve himself or give himself the last anointing. The grace of God comes to us through the community into which we are incorporated through baptism.

In the passage from St Mark, Christ compares the community which he has gathered about him to a family; or rather, he says that they, not his blood-relations, are his real family. Faith and obedience to Christ's teaching create a real spiritual relationship between his disciples. All share in his teaching, his life and his spirit. St Paul describes this spirit as one of charity, joy and peace: Christ, who is always secretly present and active among his disciples, teaches us to restrain our aggressiveness, to avoid hurting one another, and so to live in love and peace.

Within Christ's family there is interaction of one member upon another, for, as St Paul says, not all have the same gifts. If this interaction is welcomed in a spirit of cooperation and not rejected in a spirit of rivalry, the body is built up and grows strong. We should not regret the necessity of membership of the Church or wish we could follow a solitary way to God. We should positively want to receive the grace, instruction, admonition, comfort and encouragement which Christ offers us through the lives and words of our fellow men.

In the realm of Christ's grace, the generations should not be in conflict with one another. Christ placed a child in the midst of his disciples to teach them a lesson in humility. When the older generation teaches the younger with reverence, the younger is less likely to rebel and reject. The Church, like any family, is composed of many members of varied age and varied talents, but from this diversity there can arise a harmonious unity within which all, in their different ways, reflect the likeness of Christ (cf 2 Cor 3:18).

Prayer

Give us the humility and discernment, O Lord, to recognise in your Church the family and household of your chosen disciples; and preserve us from the snare of disillusionment.

30

BELIEVING AND SEEING

The Faith of a Gentile is rewarded

As Jesus entered Capernaum, a centurion came forward to him, beseeching him and saying, "Lord, my servant is lying paralyzed at home, in terrible distress." And he said to him, "I will come and heal him." But the centurion answered him, "Lord, I am not worthy to have you come under my roof; but only say the word, and my servant will be healed. For I am a man under authority, with soldiers under me; and I say to one, 'Go,' and he goes, and to another, 'Come,' and he comes, and to my slave, 'Do this,' and he does it." When Jesus heard him, he marvelled, and said to those who followed him, "Truly, I say to you, not even in Israel have I found such faith. I tell you, many will come from east and west and sit at table with Abraham, Isaac, and Jacob in the kingdom of heaven, while the sons of the kingdom will be thrown into the outer darkness; there men will weep and gnash their teeth." And to the centurion Jesus said, "Go; be it done for you as you have believed." And the servant was healed at that very moment.

And when Jesus entered Peter's house, he saw his mother-in-law lying sick with a fever; he touched her hand, and the fever left her, and she rose and served him. That evening they brought to him many who were possessed with demons; and he cast out the spirits with a word, and

healed all who were sick. This was to fulfil what was spoken by the prophet Isaiah, "He took our infirmities and bore our diseases."

(Mt 8:5-17)

Faith is put to a Test

Jesus came again to Cana in Galilee, where he had made the water wine. And at Capernaum there was an official whose son was ill. When he heard that Jesus had come from Judea to Galilee, he went and begged him to come down and heal his son, for he was at the point of death. Jesus therefore said to him, "Unless you see signs and wonders you will not believe." The official said to him, "Sir, come down before my child dies." Jesus said to him, "Go; your son will live." The man believed the word that Jesus spoke to him and went his way. As he was going down, his servants met him and told him that his son was living. So he asked them the hour when he began to mend, and they said to him, "Yesterday at the seventh hour the fever left him." The father knew that was the hour when Jesus had said to him, "Your son will live"; and he himself believed, and all his household.

(Jn 4:46-53)

Reflection

It is very easy to misread this passage from St John. If you make Jesus say, 'Unless you see *signs* and *wonders,* you will not believe,' he seems to disapprove of miracles and say that faith should not rest on them. Yet he did many miracles! The correct way to read it is, I am sure, "Unless you *see* signs and wonders, you will not believe.' The emphatic words, as often in St John, are seeing and believing. 'Blessed are those who have not seen and have believed.' Jesus expected people to believe the reports of his miracles (and later of his resurrection) and *therefore* to believe in him. 'Blessed are those who have not seen and have believed'

means 'Blessed are those who have not seen miracles worked, but have believed those who have seen them.'

However, this miracle shows that it can also mean: 'Blessed are those who have not yet seen, and have nevertheless believed; for they will see.' The ruler's faith is put to a test. Jesus says: 'Go, your son lives,' and, the text says, 'the man believed the word.' Our faith is put to a similar test every time we receive a sacrament: if we believe the word, it has its effect, and one day we shall know that it is so.

Why is it that God makes our salvation depend on faith in this way—on faith in the reports of other men about what Jesus said and did? I suspect it may be to restore the virtue of fidelity among mankind. It is endlessly said and sung that love or charity binds a community together. But equally important is faith or fidelity: the members must trust one another's word. When Jesus appeared after the resurrection, he rebuked those of his disciples who had not believed the ones who had seen him risen—they *ought* to have believed then.

Thank God, we have persevered thus far in believing the words of Christ's disciples. Faith is on test, and the test can get harder as time goes on and faith loses its newness. That is why we should always pray for perseverance—and be on our watch, not only against downright disbelief, but against murmuring and timidity. We strengthen our faith by exercising it in prayer, and by acting upon it. Make sure that you do something today, which you would not have done, if you had not been Christ's disciple.

Prayer

Give us the grace, O Lord, to persevere and to complete the journey on which we have embarked under your guidance. Bring us safely to port in the new world which you have prepared for those who obey the gospel.

31

THE GIFT OF AUTHORITY

The Council of Jerusalem

The apostles and the elders were gathered together for consultation; and after there had been much debate, Peter rose and said to them, "Brethren, you know that in the early days God made choice among you, that by my mouth the Gentiles should hear the word of the gospel and believe. And God who knows the heart bore witness to them, giving them the Holy Spirit just as he did to us; and he made no distinction between us and them, but cleansed their hearts by faith. Now therefore why do you make trial of God by putting a yoke upon the neck of the disciples which neither our fathers nor we have been able to bear? But we believe that we shall be saved through the grace of the Lord Jesus, just as they will."

And all the assembly kept silence; and they listened to Barnabas and Paul as they related what signs and wonders God had done through them among the Gentiles. After they finished speaking, James replied, "Brethren, listen to me. Symeon has related how God first visited the Gentiles, to take out of them a people for his name. And with this the words of the prophets agree, as it is written, 'After this I will return, and I will rebuild the dwelling of David, which has fallen; I will rebuild its ruins, and I will set it up, that the rest of men may seek the Lord, and all the Gentiles who are called by my name, says the Lord, who has made these things known from of old.'

Therefore my judgment is that we should not trouble those of the Gentiles who turn to God, but should write to them to abstain from the pollutions of idols and from unchastity and from what is strangled and from blood. For from early generations Moses has had in every city those who preach him, for he is read every sabbath in the synagogues."

Then it seemed good to the apostles and the elders, with the whole church, to choose men from among them and send them to Antioch with Paul and Barnabas. They sent Judas called Barsabbas, and Silas, leading men among the brethren, with the following letter: "The brethren, both the apostles and the elders, to the brethren who are of the Gentiles in Antioch and Syria and Cilicia, greeting. Since we have heard that some persons from us have troubled you with words, unsettling your minds, although we gave them no instructions, it has seemed good to us in assembly to choose men and send them to you with our beloved Barnabas and Paul, men who have risked their lives for the sake of our Lord Jesus Christ. We have therefore sent Judas and Silas, who themselves will tell you the same things by word of mouth. For it has seemed good to the Holy Spirit and to us to lay upon you no greater burden than these necessary things: that you abstain from what has been sacrificed to idols and from blood and from what is strangled and from unchastity. If you keep yourselves from these, you will do well. Farewell."

(Acts 15:6-29)

The Authority of Peter

When Jesus came into the district of Caesarea Philippi, he asked his disciples, "Who do men say that the Son of man is?" And they said, "Some say John the Baptist, others say Elijah, and others Jeremiah or one of the prophets." He said to them, "But who do you say that I am?" Simon Peter replied, "You are the Christ, the Son of the living

God." And Jesus answered him, "Blessed are you, Simon Bar-Jona! For flesh and blood has not revealed this to you, but my Father who is in heaven. And I tell you, you are Peter, and on this rock I will build my church, and the powers of death shall not prevail against it. I will give you the keys of the kingdom of heaven, and whatever you bind on earth shall be bound in heaven, and whatever you loose on earth shall be loosed in heaven." Then he strictly charged the disciples to tell no one that he was the Christ.

(Mt 16:13-20)

Reflection

Jewish teachers of Christ's day did not claim personal authority as he did. They resolved disputed points of law by quoting the decisions of certain interpreters whom they regarded as wiser than themselves. What was most new and original in the preaching of Jesus was his authority: 'It was said to the men of old... but I say to you...' He does not set aside the law of Moses, but he does give an authoritative interpretation which can, in effect, abrogate a particular law, such as Moses' regulations for the procedure in divorce.

Jesus bequeathed his authority to his disciples (cf Lk 22:30) and in particular to St Peter, and promised that their decisions would be endorsed in heaven. By settling disputed points within the Church, they would preserve peace and unity, and mark out the way of God for disciples to follow. In the reading from the Acts of the Apostles, we see how they resolved the dispute which arose at Antioch over the obligations to be laid upon Gentile converts.

It was important for the disciples' peace of mind that such authority should exist in the Church. Jesus warned his hearers that salvation is not easy; the many who are content to follow their own permissive consciences are on the broad road to perdition (cf Mt 7:13-14). The

disciples and their successors have authority to specify just what is required for admission to the kingdom. Remembering no doubt that Jesus had described his yoke as an easy one (Mt 11:30), the disciples at the Council of Jerusalem decided not to impose upon Gentile converts the whole burden of Jewish law. In their decretal letter they assure Gentile converts that this is not necessary for salvation.

The authority of the disciples is still present and operative in the Church. If we sometimes feel that it is too exacting, that may be a sign that our own standards are too lax. By listening to the teaching of others before we form our own consciences, we expose ourselves to the influence of the Holy Spirit working through other members of the same Body. In this way our minds are renewed, and we grow into that mind which was and is in Christ Jesus.

Prayer

Guide the minds of our rulers, Lord Jesus, so that they may care for your flock with love and gentleness; inspire them to set a good example, so that their brethren will follow them willingly.

32

FAITH IN GOD'S PROMISES

Faith merges with Hope

Without faith it is impossible to please God. For whoever would draw near to God must believe that he exists and that he rewards those who seek him. By faith Noah, being warned by God concerning events as yet unseen, took heed and constructed an ark for the saving of his household; by this he condemned the world and became an heir of the righteousness which comes by faith.

By faith Abraham obeyed when he was called to go out to a place which he was to receive as an inheritance; and he went out, not knowing where he was to go. By faith he sojourned in the land of promise, as in a foreign land, living in tents with Isaac and Jacob, heirs with him of the same promise. For he looked forward to the city which has foundations, whose builder and maker is God.

(Heb 11:6-10)

Who will see God?

"Blessed are the poor in spirit, for theirs is the kingdom of heaven. Blessed are those who mourn, for they shall be comforted. Blessed are the meek, for they shall inherit the earth. Blessed are those who hunger and thirst for righteousness, for they shall be satisfied. Blessed are the merciful, for they shall obtain mercy. Blessed are the pure in heart, for they shall see God. Blessed are the peacemakers,

for they shall be called sons of God. Blessed are those who are persecuted for righteousness' sake, for theirs is the kingdom of heaven."

(Mt 5:3-10)

Reflection

Faith is our response to God's words of revelation: it is the response which he moves us to make to his commands and to his promises. Since promises refer to the future, our faith in God's promises is almost identical with hope. God beckons us into a future which he has planned for us. He is 'the God of hope,' because what he has planned for us is good.

In the beatitudes Christ promises us admission to the kingdom and the vision of God. What exactly this will mean we do not know. We have been given no detailed description of the life of the world to come. We can make a guess perhaps from the story of the man born blind: when his eyes were opened, he entered into a new world of colour, light, beauty, and richer personal relationships; he saw the earthly Jerusalem and its temple, God's priests and his worshippers. We who now see the heavenly Jerusalem and its temple only by faith, will one day receive the light of glory, and our faith will give place to vision.

Meanwhile, we live in faith and hope. We accept and welcome the promises contained in the second halves of the beatitudes, and therefore try to live in the spirit of Christ described in the first halves. We strive to become Christ-like in order to be fit for admission into the kingdom —so that we will 'belong' there.

The hopes and fears that centre upon judgment affect our conduct probably far more than we realize. We are *not* content to settle down in this world and make ourselves as comfortable as we can, because the years slip by, and we know that the kingdom is at hand—for those who have

tried to live worthily. The Holy Spirit, the royal power of Christ, is already at work in us, making us groan with dissatisfaction for this world and longing for the world to come. We do not know what it will be; but God our Father is good to us. Therefore we can look forward to it as a homecoming. In this too we imitate Jesus who rejoiced at the thought of his return to the Father.

Prayer

Strengthen in us, O Lord, the faith you have given us; and awaken in our hearts a lively desire for the fulfilment of your promises.

33

FAITH AND VISION

Blessed are the Pure of Heart

Finally, brethren, we beseech and exhort you in the Lord Jesus, that as you learned from us how you ought to live and to please God, just as you are doing, you do so more and more. For you know what instructions we gave you through the Lord Jesus. For this is the will of God, your sanctification: that you abstain from immorality; that each one of you know how to control his own body in holiness and honour, not in the passion of lust like heathen who do not know God; that no man transgress, and wrong his brother in this matter, because the Lord is an avenger in all these things, as we solemnly forewarned you. For God has not called us for uncleanness, but in holiness.

(1 Thes 4:1-7)

A Preview of Heaven

After six days Jesus took with him Peter and James and John his brother, and led them up a high mountain apart. And he was transfigured before them, and his face shone like the sun, and his garments became white as light. And behold, there appeared to them Moses and Elijah, talking with him. And Peter said to Jesus, "Lord, it is well that we are here; if you wish, I will make three booths here, one for you and one for Moses and one for Elijah. He was still speaking, when lo, a bright cloud overshadowed them,

and a voice from the cloud said, "This is my beloved Son, with whom I am well pleased; listen to him." When the disciples heard this, they fell on their faces, and were filled with awe. But Jesus came and touched them, saying, "Rise, and have no fear." And when they lifted up their eyes, they saw no one but Jesus only.

And as they were coming down the mountain, Jesus commanded them, "Tell no one the vision, until the Son of man is raised from the dead."

(Mt 17:1-9)

Reflection

Among all the incidents narrated in the gospel before or after the resurrection, the transfiguration is quite exceptional. Elsewhere, Jesus looks like any other man. After curing the paralytic at Bethsaida he simply disappeared into the crowd; in Gethsemane Judas had to give a special sign to distinguish him among his apostles. After the resurrection, in the garden, on the road to Emmaus, and at the lakeside, he is mistaken for a gardener, a wayfarer and a beggar. But in the transfiguration, he is seen for a while in his glory—and the three disciples are overwhelmed.

What was the purpose of this extraordinary incident? Some of the Fathers conjectured that the disciples were granted this vision to prepare them for the passion, so that they would not lose faith when they saw Jesus rejected and executed as a criminal. But if that was the purpose, the transfiguration failed of its effect—because during the passion the disciples did not remain faithful: none of them died with him; all ran away; Peter denied him. And their faith was restored, not by the memory of any incident during his public ministry, but by the resurrection appearances.

Perhaps, then, it is better to look upon the transfiguration as a preview of the glory which Christ has in the

kingdom of heaven, and as an incentive to hope. The three disciples saw the glory that was always present in Christ's body, though concealed throughout his ministry and passion. And they saw in the figures of Moses and Elijah how they themselves would share in Christ's glory and be transfigured along with him. It was a revelation in vision of what they already held in faith. The people of Nazareth, who put no faith in Jesus, asked: 'Where did he get this wisdom, and these powers? Is he not the son of Joseph the carpenter?' The disciples knew by faith that he had received this wisdom and these powers from his heavenly Father. In the transfiguration they were allowed to *see* what it meant that the fulness of the Godhead dwelled in him corporally .

The vision was a revelation of Christ (cf 2 Pet 1:16-19), and at the same time a revelation about themselves, and about all disciples. Already we share in the glory of Christ, already 'we are being changed into his likeness from one degree of glory to another' (2 Cor 3:18); but this transfiguration of our being is hidden, as his glory was hidden during his earthly life. One day it will be revealed—and we shall be like him, as Moses and Elijah were like him. Our bodies too will be revealed as temples of the divine glory. That is why, as St Paul says in his Epistle, we must keep them pure and chaste and free from all defilement.

Prayer

Cleanse us, O Lord, from our sins, that we may be made worthy to enter your presence, to see your majesty, and to reflect in our own persons your beauty and your glory.

BIBLE PASSAGES USED

Old Testament

Gen 1:24-28;2:15-17	page	9
Gen 22:1-12	"	63
Exod 3:16-17;4:1-9	"	32
Exod 19:1-6;20:1-2	"	28
1 Kgs 19:9-12	"	35
Job 38:1-11;40:3-5	page	22
Eccles 8:8-15	"	57
Isa 2:2-4	"	94
Jer 31:31-34	"	97

New Testament

Mt 5:3-10	page	110
Mt 5:13-16	"	94
Mt 5:43-48	"	45
Mt 6:26-30	"	10
Mt 8:5-13	"	22
Mt 8:5-17	"	103
Mt 8:23-27	"	48
Mt 11:25-30	"	39
Mt 11:27-30	"	60
Mt 16:13-20	"	107
Mt 17:1-9	"	113
Mt 19:3-11	"	88
Mt 24:45-51	"	58
Mt 26:57-70	"	51
Mt 27:51-54	"	43
Mk 3:31-35	"	100
Lk 1:30-38	"	64
Lk 11:14-28	"	28
Lk 18:31-43	"	75
Jn 3:1-16	"	81
Jn 3:11-17	"	13
Jn 4:46-53	"	104
Jn 5:1-14	"	91
Jn 6:35-40	"	54
Jn 8:21-27	"	33
Jn 8:31-36	"	25
Jn 9:14-34	"	70
Jn 11:21-27	"	78
Jn 11:38-44	"	19
Jn 14:1-11	"	67
Jn 14:23-27	"	36
Jn 16:4-14	page	85
Jn 20:19-23	"	97
Jn 20:26-31	"	16
Acts 2:1-11	"	35
Acts 2:22-37	"	42
Acts 15:6-29	"	106
Acts 17:22-31	"	12
Acts 22:6-21	"	38
Rom 1:18-23	"	19
Rom 9:1-6	"	70
Rom 12:4-8	"	100
1 Cor 1:18-25	"	81
1 Cor 2:6-13	"	60
1 Cor 7:12-17	"	88
1 Cor 13:1-13	"	74
1 Cor 13:9-12	"	67
1 Cor 15:51-58	"	54
Gal 3:1-5	"	16
Gal 3:21-26	"	25
1 Thes 4:1-7	"	113
1 Tim 3:14-16	"	85
Tit 2:11-14	"	45
Heb 2:10-15	"	48
Heb 9:11-14	"	91
Heb 11:6-10	"	110
Heb 11:24-27	"	51
1 Jn 5:1-5	"	78

2758 1

4-15-76